Contrarian

Bacon

Contrarian

Bacon

Earl Jay

outskirts press

Contrarian Bacon

v1.0 r1.0

Outskirts Press, Inc.
http://www.outskirtspress.com

ISBN: 978-1-9772-3369-1

PRINTED IN THE UNITED STATES OF AMERICA

Introduction

Discipline last because it's the only thing that works. (Try everything else for experience.) This book is intended to be consumed daily and is suggestive rather than explanatory. While traditional dietary nutrition is critical in maintaining a healthy lifestyle, I wrote this book to focus more on mental nutrition with a sarcastic spin on mainstream habits. I currently have many influences that I could mention or reference in specific situations, but I am not going to do it. This is my work and my work alone; Google has no place here. This is the first book I have written from cover to cover, so if you're looking for any kind of familiar writing style or technique you will not find it within these pages. What you will find is a unique individual perspective on circumstances that many of us will come across eventually and how to leverage just about any experience for personal benefit. I have no idea where you are in life professionally, mentally, or spiritually; but I do know if you have taken the time to secure a copy of this book that you are interested in learning and that is worth celebrating. Two components of this book are brevity and clarity. Time is our greatest asset and I'm not going to waste it attempting to prove to you that I'm a genius because I'm not. I am, however, taking a contrarian approach to writing a book meaning I am attempting something that has never been done, luckily I'm pretty good at marketing and will have hundreds if not thousands of pre orders before I print any physical copies. Believe it or not I'm not writing this book for money—my motivation is simply to assist individuals who wish to improve their lives by committing to 3 daily mental meals and a snack. Not going to lie, this is the worst I have seen things in my young life, which is why I feel slightly responsible for some of the things going on right now. I've always had a strong work ethic and the ability to create revenue streams, yet somehow, I don't feel as if I can relax just yet. As I mentioned previously this is my first real attempt at writing and publishing a book. I'm paying for the printing and any other publishing services but every other part of the process will be done by me personally because it is truly sell or be sold and I'm not impressed by anything in the literary world at the moment other than my desire to be the change I would like to see. But the beauty of it all is that this book has nothing to do with me and everything to do with how you, the reader, receive the content I have produced. Disclaimer: this book is not for everybody. In fact, it is for you and you alone until you feel confident enough to write a book yourself or teach the daily lessons to others in a meaningful way. The biggest secret is that there are no secrets. As we begin this remember that momentum requires action. This book is truly about the reader and I am simply authoring a book I wish I had ten years ago. To get the most out of this book it will help if you know how to use your imagination. We don't need to make everyday a masterpiece, but it certainly helps in the long run. All we have is now, which is the perfect time to commit to studying/learning, practicing, and training patterns of the mind. If you have managed to find a craft that you can apply this information to, great! If not even better, because you likely won't have to unlearn as many outdated life strategies. I've had the opportunity to experience highly efficient systems up close and see what works for given situations. I have also had the luxury of witnessing complete fiascos that operate as if nothing is wrong. It is my hope that this book is the little nudge you need to see things as they are and approach situations with a first-or-last mentality, and believe it or not being last sometimes is the best thing you could ask for which is why this book is titled *Contrarian Bacon;* I can't lose even if I wanted to and you're in the same boat with a better view and fancy refreshments.

COMPOUND INTEREST FORMULA

$$A = P\left(1 + \frac{r}{n}\right)^{nt}$$

A = final amount

P = initial principle balance

r = interest rate

n = number of times interest applied per time period

t = number of time periods elapsed

How to use this book:

Consume each daily message when desired. Contrarian cards optional.

Caution: Do not read this book in one sitting. Each daily message when properly consumed and mentally digested will act as an illuminating guide through your current circumstance. If this is not a fun process for you, send me my damn book back and go lick public toilet seats.

Use the journaling reflection sections for deeper understanding and retention.

Geocoding locations are Contrarian hot spots, meaning go at your own risk; no guarantees here folks, and remember to have patience.

Charts and formulas are suggestive and probably won't work for you individually for a couple years, but don't quit, in fact buy another copy of this book and help me get richer.

Any and all laughter from this book is monitored using advanced technology and charged to whatever payment method you used to purchase this book.

100 Days of Gratitude

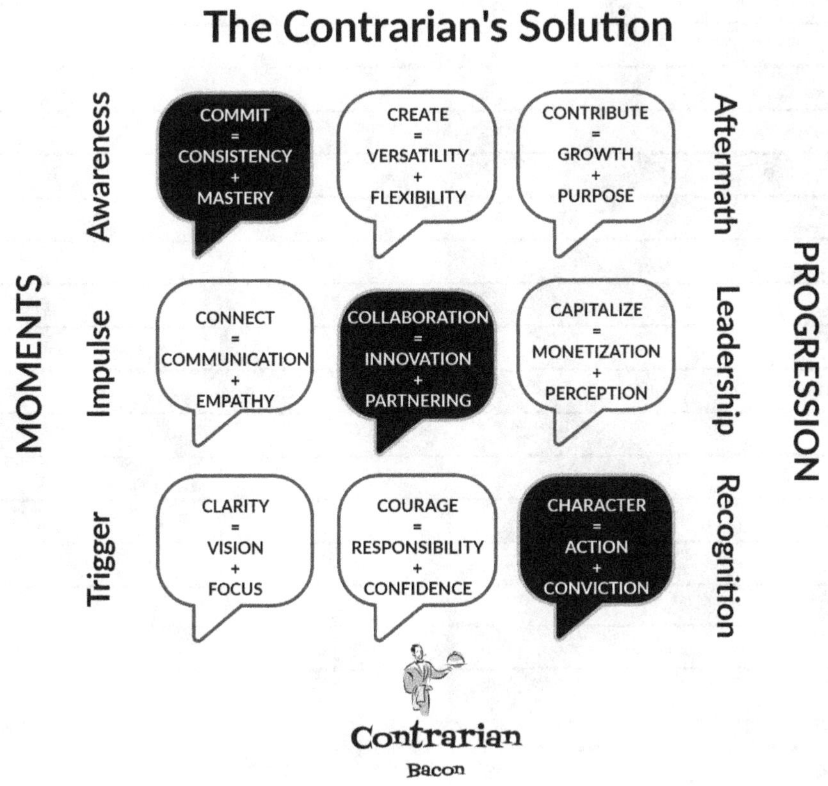
The Contrarian's Solution
MOMENTS
Awareness
Impulse
Trigger
PROGRESSION
Aftermath
Leadership
Recognition
COMMIT = CONSISTENCY + MASTERY
CREATE = VERSATILITY + FLEXIBILITY
CONTRIBUTE = GROWTH + PURPOSE
CONNECT = COMMUNICATION + EMPATHY
COLLABORATION = INNOVATION + PARTNERING
CAPITALIZE = MONETIZATION + PERCEPTION
CLARITY = VISION + FOCUS
COURAGE = RESPONSIBILITY + CONFIDENCE
CHARACTER = ACTION + CONVICTION
Contrarian
Bacon

DAY 1

Breakfast: A small daily dose of gratitude has no side effects.

Lunch: Gratitude is less expensive than regret.

Dinner: Noise is needed but gratitude can be quickly found in silence.

Snack: Focus on gratitude until you hate it or love it.

Misplaced Focus		Negative Result	Redirected Focus		Positive Result
#1: Doubt	◆»	Paralysis	Presence	◆»	Passion
#2: Complacency	◆»	Pain	Engagement	◆»	Positive Expectation
#3 Blame	◆»	Powerlessness/ Problems	Resourcefulness	◆»	Possibilities
#4 Indecision	◆»	Procrastination	Action	◆»	Progress
#5: Selfishness	◆»	Guilt	Service	◆»	Peace of Mind

DAY 2

Breakfast: Gratitude is the least complex emotion.

Lunch: In unfamiliar situations let gratitude be your reasoning voice.

Dinner: Don't forget the gratitude.

Snack: If presence needed a foundation gratitude might work.

Misplaced Focus	Negative Result	Redirected Focus	Positive Result
#1: Doubt	Paralysis	Presence	Passion
#2: Complacency	Pain	Engagement	Positive Expectation
#3 Blame	Powerlessness/ Problems	Resourcefulness	Possibilities
#4 Indecision	Procrastination	Action	Progress
#5: Selfishness	Guilt	Service	Peace of Mind

DAY 3

Breakfast: Gratitude both ways before crossing the street.

Lunch: Choose gratitude more than solitude.

Dinner: Oh shit, I lost my gratitude.

Snack: Gratitude likes to hang with success but doesn't trust the relationship.

Misplaced Focus		Negative Result	Redirected Focus		Positive Result
#1: Doubt	»	Paralysis	Presence	»	Passion
#2: Complacency	»	Pain	Engagement	»	Positive Expectation
#3 Blame	»	Powerlessness/ Problems	Resourcefulness	»	Possibilities
#4 Indecision	»	Procrastination	Action	»	Progress
#5: Selfishness	»	Guilt	Service	»	Peace of Mind

DAY 4

Breakfast: Everything in moderation unless gratitude is involved.

Lunch: Eat, sleep, gratitude.

Dinner: The longer you live the more relevant gratitude is.

Snack: I farted, and it smells like gratitude.

Misplaced Focus		Negative Result	Redirected Focus		Positive Result
#1: Doubt	◆》	Paralysis	Presence	◆》	Passion
#2: Complacency	◆》	Pain	Engagement	◆》	Positive Expectation
#3 Blame	◆》	Powerlessness/ Problems	Resourcefulness	◆》	Possibilities
#4 Indecision	◆》	Procrastination	Action	◆》	Progress
#5: Selfishness	◆》	Guilt	Service	◆》	Peace of Mind

DAY 5

Breakfast: Gratitude isn't everything but it's right up there with oxygen.

Lunch: Pace yourself—gratitude is not about speed.

Dinner: Between gratitude and grief you will find the best balance.

Snack: All that exists is principle, process, and gratitude peeking around the corner.

Misplaced Focus		Negative Result	Redirected Focus		Positive Result
#1: Doubt	◆》	Paralysis	Presence	◆》	Passion
#2: Complacency	◆》	Pain	Engagement	◆》	Positive Expectation
#3 Blame	◆》	Powerlessness/ Problems	Resourcefulness	◆》	Possibilities
#4 Indecision	◆》	Procrastination	Action	◆》	Progress
#5: Selfishness	◆》	Guilt	Service	◆》	Peace of Mind

DAY 6

Breakfast: One of the most random things you can do is practice gratitude for no reason.

Lunch: Gratitude first, ask questions later.

Dinner: "Thank you" awakens gratitude.

Snack: Gratitude quotes don't work well when in doubt.

Misplaced Focus		Negative Result	Redirected Focus		Positive Result
#1: Doubt	⟫	Paralysis	Presence	⟫	Passion
#2: Complacency	⟫	Pain	Engagement	⟫	Positive Expectation
#3 Blame	⟫	Powerlessness/ Problems	Resourcefulness	⟫	Possibilities
#4 Indecision	⟫	Procrastination	Action	⟫	Progress
#5: Selfishness	⟫	Guilt	Service	⟫	Peace of Mind

DAY 7

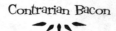

Breakfast: The attitude does not fall far from the tree with or without gratitude.

Lunch: Annoyances occur when gratitude takes a break.

Dinner: Luck has nothing to do with gratitude.

Snack: Gratitude is the code we should all live by.

Misplaced Focus		Negative Result	Redirected Focus		Positive Result
#1: Doubt	◆》	Paralysis	Presence	◆》	Passion
#2: Complacency	◆》	Pain	Engagement	◆》	Positive Expectation
#3 Blame	◆》	Powerlessness/ Problems	Resourcefulness	◆》	Possibilities
#4 Indecision	◆》	Procrastination	Action	◆》	Progress
#5: Selfishness	◆》	Guilt	Service	◆》	Peace of Mind

DAY 8

Breakfast: Gratitude is life's natural enhancer.

Lunch: Failure is a result of not understanding gratitude.

Dinner: It is challenging to try everything while excluding gratitude.

Snack: Gratitude is the warmth of a cold world.

Misplaced Focus		Negative Result	Redirected Focus		Positive Result
#1: Doubt	◆》	Paralysis	Presence	◆》	Passion
#2: Complacency	◆》	Pain	Engagement	◆》	Positive Expectation
#3 Blame	◆》	Powerlessness/ Problems	Resourcefulness	◆》	Possibilities
#4 Indecision	◆》	Procrastination	Action	◆》	Progress
#5: Selfishness	◆》	Guilt	Service	◆》	Peace of Mind

DAY 9

Breakfast: Having gratitude does not require good credit.

Lunch: When people say anything is possible gratitude smiles.

Dinner: A change of direction is more likely to produce gratitude than a smoothly planned trip.

Snack: Championships require gratitude.

Misplaced Focus		Negative Result	Redirected Focus		Positive Result
#1: Doubt	◆》	Paralysis	Presence	◆》	Passion
#2: Complacency	◆》	Pain	Engagement	◆》	Positive Expectation
#3 Blame	◆》	Powerlessness/ Problems	Resourcefulness	◆》	Possibilities
#4 Indecision	◆》	Procrastination	Action	◆》	Progress
#5: Selfishness	◆》	Guilt	Service	◆》	Peace of Mind

DAY 10

Breakfast: Gratitude is made in the soul.

Lunch: Gratitude is a cool breeze in the heat of the moment.

Dinner: We are surrounded by intelligence but
still live with conflict; study gratitude.

Snack: Quitters completely ignore gratitude.

Misplaced Focus		Negative Result	Redirected Focus		Positive Result
#1: Doubt	◆》	Paralysis	Presence	◆》	Passion
#2: Complacency	◆》	Pain	Engagement	◆》	Positive Expectation
#3 Blame	◆》	Powerlessness/ Problems	Resourcefulness	◆》	Possibilities
#4 Indecision	◆》	Procrastination	Action	◆》	Progress
#5: Selfishness	◆》	Guilt	Service	◆》	Peace of Mind

DAY 11

Breakfast: Gratitude should be paid in full.

Lunch: If it scares you, do it with gratitude.

Dinner: Gratitude, gratitude, and more gratitude.

Snack: Gratitude is a cure for manipulation.

Misplaced Focus		Negative Result	Redirected Focus		Positive Result
#1: Doubt	◆》	Paralysis	Presence	◆》	Passion
#2: Complacency	◆》	Pain	Engagement	◆》	Positive Expectation
#3 Blame	◆》	Powerlessness/ Problems	Resourcefulness	◆》	Possibilities
#4 Indecision	◆》	Procrastination	Action	◆》	Progress
#5: Selfishness	◆》	Guilt	Service	◆》	Peace of Mind

DAY 12

Breakfast: Treat people like people for gratitude's sake.

Lunch: I thought about using a sentence without gratitude and my cell phone died; not going to do it anymore.

Dinner: Profanity when used properly is the purest form of gratitude.

Snack: When America finds out about gratitude, the Constitution will make sense.

Misplaced Focus	Negative Result	Redirected Focus	Positive Result
#1: Doubt	Paralysis	Presence	Passion
#2: Complacency	Pain	Engagement	Positive Expectation
#3 Blame	Powerlessness/ Problems	Resourcefulness	Possibilities
#4 Indecision	Procrastination	Action	Progress
#5: Selfishness	Guilt	Service	Peace of Mind

DAY 13

Breakfast: Unfortunately, gratitude is easily distracted.

Lunch: Hatred discovered gratitude and just like that jealousy was spawned into existence.

Dinner: If I were writing this in jail or a fully loaded bank vault my focus would be gratitude.

Snack: If you ever want to outwork me master gratitude, then give up.

Misplaced Focus	Negative Result	Redirected Focus	Positive Result
#1: Doubt	Paralysis	Presence	Passion
#2: Complacency	Pain	Engagement	Positive Expectation
#3 Blame	Powerlessness/ Problems	Resourcefulness	Possibilities
#4 Indecision	Procrastination	Action	Progress
#5: Selfishness	Guilt	Service	Peace of Mind

DAY 14

Breakfast: I have 99 problems, but gratitude isn't one.

Lunch: The rule-book neglects gratitude.

Dinner: Hold my gratitude and watch this.

Snack: Most achievement overlooks gratitude for obvious reasons.

Misplaced Focus		Negative Result	Redirected Focus		Positive Result
#1: Doubt	◆》	Paralysis	Presence	◆》	Passion
#2: Complacency	◆》	Pain	Engagement	◆》	Positive Expectation
#3 Blame	◆》	Powerlessness/ Problems	Resourcefulness	◆》	Possibilities
#4 Indecision	◆》	Procrastination	Action	◆》	Progress
#5: Selfishness	◆》	Guilt	Service	◆》	Peace of Mind

DAY 15

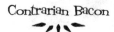

Breakfast: People who can criticize gratitude are special; thank them and carry on.

Lunch: How can I use gratitude to avoid depression or anxiety today?

Dinner: Gratitude>Motivation.

Snack: Stagnant gratitude is what myths are made of.

Misplaced Focus		Negative Result	Redirected Focus		Positive Result
#1: Doubt	»	Paralysis	Presence	»	Passion
#2: Complacency	»	Pain	Engagement	»	Positive Expectation
#3 Blame	»	Powerlessness/ Problems	Resourcefulness	»	Possibilities
#4 Indecision	»	Procrastination	Action	»	Progress
#5: Selfishness	»	Guilt	Service	»	Peace of Mind

DAY 16

Breakfast: Focusing on negativity increases demand for gratitude.

Lunch: Better is sponsored by gratitude.

Dinner: Gratitude sleeps with peace of mind.

Snack: Persist long enough and gratitude becomes the only option.

Misplaced Focus		Negative Result	Redirected Focus		Positive Result
#1: Doubt	◆》	Paralysis	Presence	◆》	Passion
#2: Complacency	◆》	Pain	Engagement	◆》	Positive Expectation
#3 Blame	◆》	Powerlessness/ Problems	Resourcefulness	◆》	Possibilities
#4 Indecision	◆》	Procrastination	Action	◆》	Progress
#5: Selfishness	◆》	Guilt	Service	◆》	Peace of Mind

DAY 17

Breakfast: Perfection can defeat gratitude. If that doesn't scare you nothing will.

Lunch: Writing is so painful to me that gratitude was the only answer.

Dinner: Solutions rooted in gratitude are boring but effective.

Snack: Alcohol consumption breeds gratitude.

Misplaced Focus		Negative Result	Redirected Focus		Positive Result
#1: Doubt	◆»	Paralysis	Presence	◆»	Passion
#2: Complacency	◆»	Pain	Engagement	◆»	Positive Expectation
#3 Blame	◆»	Powerlessness/ Problems	Resourcefulness	◆»	Possibilities
#4 Indecision	◆»	Procrastination	Action	◆»	Progress
#5: Selfishness	◆»	Guilt	Service	◆»	Peace of Mind

DAY 18

Breakfast: This gratitude stuff might work.

Lunch: If gratitude alone were responsible for paying salaries, we would be all set.

Dinner: Believe it or not gratitude is a hip-hop fan.

Snack: Any great discovery is the latest and greatest prank coordinated by gratitude.

Misplaced Focus	Negative Result	Redirected Focus	Positive Result
#1: Doubt	Paralysis	Presence	Passion
#2: Complacency	Pain	Engagement	Positive Expectation
#3 Blame	Powerlessness/ Problems	Resourcefulness	Possibilities
#4 Indecision	Procrastination	Action	Progress
#5: Selfishness	Guilt	Service	Peace of Mind

DAY 19

Breakfast: If you're having trouble locating gratitude, check your spam folder.

Lunch: Gratitude needs permission to go outside and play.

Dinner: Confusion can travel around the world 3 times before gratitude has biscuits and tea.

Snack: Look around: do you notice anything that might involve gratitude?

Misplaced Focus		Negative Result	Redirected Focus		Positive Result
#1: Doubt	⟫	Paralysis	Presence	⟫	Passion
#2: Complacency	⟫	Pain	Engagement	⟫	Positive Expectation
#3 Blame	⟫	Powerlessness/ Problems	Resourcefulness	⟫	Possibilities
#4 Indecision	⟫	Procrastination	Action	⟫	Progress
#5: Selfishness	⟫	Guilt	Service	⟫	Peace of Mind

DAY 20

Breakfast: More than ever before, gratitude and lifestyle are closely related.

Lunch: To the uneducated gratitude sounds like a scam.

Dinner: If gratitude were into adult entertainment,
the world would be a safer place.

Snack: If you never read another book, blame gratitude.

Misplaced Focus		Negative Result	Redirected Focus		Positive Result
#1: Doubt	◆》	Paralysis	Presence	◆》	Passion
#2: Complacency	◆》	Pain	Engagement	◆》	Positive Expectation
#3 Blame	◆》	Powerlessness/ Problems	Resourcefulness	◆》	Possibilities
#4 Indecision	◆》	Procrastination	Action	◆》	Progress
#5: Selfishness	◆》	Guilt	Service	◆》	Peace of Mind

DAY 21

Breakfast: Gratitude by example.

Lunch: If you don't wash your hands after using the bathroom, eww—gratitude won't help.

Dinner: If you ever stop learning, gratitude has nothing to do with it.

Snack: If you're not first you're going to need gratitude.

Misplaced Focus	Negative Result	Redirected Focus	Positive Result
#1: Doubt	Paralysis	Presence	Passion
#2: Complacency	Pain	Engagement	Positive Expectation
#3 Blame	Powerlessness/ Problems	Resourcefulness	Possibilities
#4 Indecision	Procrastination	Action	Progress
#5: Selfishness	Guilt	Service	Peace of Mind

DAY 22

Breakfast: To increase life expectancy practice gratitude before self-discipline.

Lunch: If it feels like work it isn't gratitude.

Dinner: Saying "I love you" without gratitude is the same as drunk texting.

Snack: Only bad will come from consistently ignoring gratitude.

Misplaced Focus		Negative Result	Redirected Focus		Positive Result
#1: Doubt	»	Paralysis	Presence	»	Passion
#2: Complacency	»	Pain	Engagement	»	Positive Expectation
#3 Blame	»	Powerlessness/ Problems	Resourcefulness	»	Possibilities
#4 Indecision	»	Procrastination	Action	»	Progress
#5: Selfishness	»	Guilt	Service	»	Peace of Mind

DAY 23

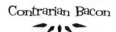

Breakfast: Relationships built from gratitude outperform rushed relationships.

Lunch: All or gratitude.

Dinner: The second you let your guard down, gratitude rewards or exposes you.

Snack: Celebrate the hardest learned lessons with gratitude.

Misplaced Focus	Negative Result	Redirected Focus	Positive Result
#1: Doubt	Paralysis	Presence	Passion
#2: Complacency	Pain	Engagement	Positive Expectation
#3 Blame	Powerlessness/ Problems	Resourcefulness	Possibilities
#4 Indecision	Procrastination	Action	Progress
#5: Selfishness	Guilt	Service	Peace of Mind

DAY 24

Breakfast: The best teachers either exclude gratitude completely or have it on display for all to see.

Lunch: It is okay to let hunger overpower gratitude occasionally.

Dinner: The feeling of gratitude is like celebrating Halloween twice a year.

Snack: Tacos are better with gratitude.

Misplaced Focus		Negative Result	Redirected Focus		Positive Result
#1: Doubt	◆》	Paralysis	Presence	◆》	Passion
#2: Complacency	◆》	Pain	Engagement	◆》	Positive Expectation
#3 Blame	◆》	Powerlessness/ Problems	Resourcefulness	◆》	Possibilities
#4 Indecision	◆》	Procrastination	Action	◆》	Progress
#5: Selfishness	◆》	Guilt	Service	◆》	Peace of Mind

DAY 25

Breakfast: If you get tired of gratitude you're one sick individual.

Lunch: Breakthroughs require more imagination than gratitude.

Dinner: Surround yourself with gratitude.

Snack: It won't always be easy, but gratitude is the most revealing burden to carry.

Misplaced Focus		Negative Result	Redirected Focus		Positive Result
#1: Doubt		Paralysis	Presence		Passion
#2: Complacency		Pain	Engagement		Positive Expectation
#3 Blame		Powerlessness/ Problems	Resourcefulness		Possibilities
#4 Indecision		Procrastination	Action		Progress
#5: Selfishness		Guilt	Service		Peace of Mind

DAY 26

Breakfast: Memories fade so that gratitude is not forgotten.

Lunch: Money comes and goes; gratitude stays and waits.

Dinner: We can agree to disagree, just not on the importance of gratitude.

Snack: Very few people will openly discuss fears of gratitude.

Misplaced Focus		Negative Result	Redirected Focus		Positive Result
#1: Doubt	◆»	Paralysis	Presence	◆»	Passion
#2: Complacency	◆»	Pain	Engagement	◆»	Positive Expectation
#3 Blame	◆»	Powerlessness/ Problems	Resourcefulness	◆»	Possibilities
#4 Indecision	◆»	Procrastination	Action	◆»	Progress
#5: Selfishness	◆»	Guilt	Service	◆»	Peace of Mind

DAY 27

Breakfast: Infants are wizards and fairies of gratitude.

Lunch: Gratitude should be prioritized over ego.

Dinner: Gratitude is a daily process.

Snack: You don't have to explain anything to anyone, especially if you believe in gratitude.

Misplaced Focus		Negative Result	Redirected Focus		Positive Result
#1: Doubt	»	Paralysis	Presence	»	Passion
#2: Complacency	»	Pain	Engagement	»	Positive Expectation
#3 Blame	»	Powerlessness/ Problems	Resourcefulness	»	Possibilities
#4 Indecision	»	Procrastination	Action	»	Progress
#5: Selfishness	»	Guilt	Service	»	Peace of Mind

DAY 28

Breakfast: There is nothing new under the sun except individual effort and the gratitude used as fuel.

Lunch: Do you have a mint or perhaps some gratitude?

Dinner: If life is a free fall, gratitude is the only hole worth falling into intentionally.

Snack: Time and space create the ideal circumstances for gratitude.

Misplaced Focus		Negative Result	Redirected Focus		Positive Result
#1: Doubt	◆》	Paralysis	Presence	◆》	Passion
#2: Complacency	◆》	Pain	Engagement	◆》	Positive Expectation
#3 Blame	◆》	Powerlessness/ Problems	Resourcefulness	◆》	Possibilities
#4 Indecision	◆》	Procrastination	Action	◆》	Progress
#5: Selfishness	◆》	Guilt	Service	◆》	Peace of Mind

DAY 29

Breakfast: Losses are natural occurrences, and gratitude is the bridge to where you wish to visit next.

Lunch: If you think too much, gratitude becomes an illusion.

Dinner: Gratitude is a useful tool to prevent the destruction of all humanity.

Snack: Gratitude is just a word that symbolizes hope to fools.

Misplaced Focus		Negative Result	Redirected Focus		Positive Result
#1: Doubt	◆》	Paralysis	Presence	◆》	Passion
#2: Complacency	◆》	Pain	Engagement	◆》	Positive Expectation
#3 Blame	◆》	Powerlessness/ Problems	Resourcefulness	◆》	Possibilities
#4 Indecision	◆》	Procrastination	Action	◆》	Progress
#5: Selfishness	◆》	Guilt	Service	◆》	Peace of Mind

DAY 30

Breakfast: Opinions make gratitude seem sketchy.

Lunch: It takes gratitude to understand people who ride rollercoasters but are afraid to drive a car.

Dinner: Precision looks dangerous when gratitude is the dominant force for too long.

Snack: Gratitude is just different.

Misplaced Focus		Negative Result	Redirected Focus		Positive Result
#1: Doubt	»	Paralysis	Presence	»	Passion
#2: Complacency	»	Pain	Engagement	»	Positive Expectation
#3 Blame	»	Powerlessness/ Problems	Resourcefulness	»	Possibilities
#4 Indecision	»	Procrastination	Action	»	Progress
#5: Selfishness	»	Guilt	Service	»	Peace of Mind

DAY 31

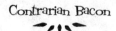

Breakfast: If you look closely, you can see gratitude in the bushes on the back of a $20 bill.

Lunch: Gratitude isn't the only way to find love, just the least painful.

Dinner: I'm currently single, but if gratitude works this one won't make it to print.

Snack: Yes, gratitude allows you to unapologetically be yourself.

Misplaced Focus		Negative Result	Redirected Focus		Positive Result
#1: Doubt	◆》	Paralysis	Presence	◆》	Passion
#2: Complacency	◆》	Pain	Engagement	◆》	Positive Expectation
#3 Blame	◆》	Powerlessness/ Problems	Resourcefulness	◆》	Possibilities
#4 Indecision	◆》	Procrastination	Action	◆》	Progress
#5: Selfishness	◆》	Guilt	Service	◆》	Peace of Mind

DAY 32

Breakfast: Island shopping requires a higher level of gratitude.

Lunch: If everybody is doing it, I seriously doubt it's gratitude.

Dinner: The harder the challenge is, the more useful gratitude is.

Snack: Even gratitude has a dark side.

Misplaced Focus	Negative Result	Redirected Focus	Positive Result
#1: Doubt	Paralysis	Presence	Passion
#2: Complacency	Pain	Engagement	Positive Expectation
#3 Blame	Powerlessness/ Problems	Resourcefulness	Possibilities
#4 Indecision	Procrastination	Action	Progress
#5: Selfishness	Guilt	Service	Peace of Mind

DAY 33

Breakfast: Aggression can surprisingly be a result of gratitude.

Lunch: Repeating the same activities for long periods of time leads to insanity or gratitude.

Dinner: Strength developed without gratitude is still strength.

Snack: Limitations occur on the blindside of gratitude.

Misplaced Focus		Negative Result	Redirected Focus		Positive Result
#1: Doubt	◆》	Paralysis	Presence	◆》	Passion
#2: Complacency	◆》	Pain	Engagement	◆》	Positive Expectation
#3 Blame	◆》	Powerlessness/ Problems	Resourcefulness	◆》	Possibilities
#4 Indecision	◆》	Procrastination	Action	◆》	Progress
#5: Selfishness	◆》	Guilt	Service	◆》	Peace of Mind

DAY 34

Breakfast: In large groups gratitude requires extreme caution.

Lunch: Simplicity is a form of ignorance that gratitude can't save.

Dinner: When a known lie seems like truth, try gratitude.

Snack: A routine is as toxic as aimlessness in certain situations; gratitude is the answer.

Misplaced Focus		Negative Result	Redirected Focus		Positive Result
#1: Doubt	»	Paralysis	Presence	»	Passion
#2: Complacency	»	Pain	Engagement	»	Positive Expectation
#3 Blame	»	Powerlessness/ Problems	Resourcefulness	»	Possibilities
#4 Indecision	»	Procrastination	Action	»	Progress
#5: Selfishness	»	Guilt	Service	»	Peace of Mind

DAY 35

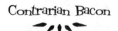

Breakfast: Most celebrities understand gratitude, they just don't talk about it.

Lunch: Done is better than perfection unless you can perfect gratitude.

Dinner: Humor has a sense of gratitude.

Snack: If you care too much, gratitude becomes manual labor.

Misplaced Focus		Negative Result	Redirected Focus		Positive Result
#1: Doubt	◆》	Paralysis	Presence	◆》	Passion
#2: Complacency	◆》	Pain	Engagement	◆》	Positive Expectation
#3 Blame	◆》	Powerlessness/ Problems	Resourcefulness	◆》	Possibilities
#4 Indecision	◆》	Procrastination	Action	◆》	Progress
#5: Selfishness	◆》	Guilt	Service	◆》	Peace of Mind

DAY 36

Breakfast: There is no way that anyone can know everything without gratitude being an educational requirement.

Lunch: Planning is the beginning of the end for gratitude.

Dinner: Awards devalue gratitude.

Snack: Gratitude is a terrible sales representative.

Misplaced Focus		Negative Result	Redirected Focus		Positive Result
#1: Doubt	◆»	Paralysis	Presence	◆»	Passion
#2: Complacency	◆»	Pain	Engagement	◆»	Positive Expectation
#3 Blame	◆»	Powerlessness/ Problems	Resourcefulness	◆»	Possibilities
#4 Indecision	◆»	Procrastination	Action	◆»	Progress
#5: Selfishness	◆»	Guilt	Service	◆»	Peace of Mind

DAY 37

Breakfast: Each individual moment eagerly awaits the opportunity to meet gratitude.

Lunch: When enough people feel you are good for society, gratitude will make more sense.

Dinner: Struggle builds unique skills and highlights gratitude.

Snack: Gratitude is an unseen danger to most.

Misplaced Focus		Negative Result	Redirected Focus		Positive Result
#1: Doubt	◆»	Paralysis	Presence	◆»	Passion
#2: Complacency	◆»	Pain	Engagement	◆»	Positive Expectation
#3 Blame	◆»	Powerlessness/ Problems	Resourcefulness	◆»	Possibilities
#4 Indecision	◆»	Procrastination	Action	◆»	Progress
#5: Selfishness	◆»	Guilt	Service	◆»	Peace of Mind

DAY 38

Breakfast: Sometimes you must give yourself a promotion and tell your boss gratitude said quit.

Lunch: Delayed gratification has gratitude written all over it.

Dinner: There is no height requirement for gratitude.

Snack: Gratitude is more how than what.

Misplaced Focus		Negative Result	Redirected Focus		Positive Result
#1: Doubt	◆»	Paralysis	Presence	◆»	Passion
#2: Complacency	◆»	Pain	Engagement	◆»	Positive Expectation
#3 Blame	◆»	Powerlessness/ Problems	Resourcefulness	◆»	Possibilities
#4 Indecision	◆»	Procrastination	Action	◆»	Progress
#5: Selfishness	◆»	Guilt	Service	◆»	Peace of Mind

DAY 39

Breakfast: If you're salvaging gratitude it's too late.

Lunch: "The faker the better" is a symptom of too much gratitude.

Dinner: Whether you commit to it or not, gratitude exists.

Snack: Short cuts are fun until gratitude sends you the bill.

Misplaced Focus		Negative Result	Redirected Focus		Positive Result
#1: Doubt	»	Paralysis	Presence	»	Passion
#2: Complacency	»	Pain	Engagement	»	Positive Expectation
#3 Blame	»	Powerlessness/ Problems	Resourcefulness	»	Possibilities
#4 Indecision	»	Procrastination	Action	»	Progress
#5: Selfishness	»	Guilt	Service	»	Peace of Mind

DAY 40

Breakfast: Take the risk or learn all you can about gratitude.

Lunch: Results don't speak, they mimic gratitude.

Dinner: The best guarantees are backed by gratitude.

Snack: The world does not need gratitude, but it certainly helps.

Misplaced Focus	Negative Result	Redirected Focus	Positive Result
#1: Doubt	Paralysis	Presence	Passion
#2: Complacency	Pain	Engagement	Positive Expectation
#3 Blame	Powerlessness/ Problems	Resourcefulness	Possibilities
#4 Indecision	Procrastination	Action	Progress
#5: Selfishness	Guilt	Service	Peace of Mind

DAY 41

Breakfast: The fragility of our existence warrants gratitude.

Lunch: You are the reason someone will learn what gratitude is.

Dinner: No matter the occasion, gratitude is the best gift to give.

Snack: Do not expect to succeed into gratitude.

Misplaced Focus		Negative Result	Redirected Focus		Positive Result
#1: Doubt	◆》	Paralysis	Presence	◆》	Passion
#2: Complacency	◆》	Pain	Engagement	◆》	Positive Expectation
#3 Blame	◆》	Powerlessness/ Problems	Resourcefulness	◆》	Possibilities
#4 Indecision	◆》	Procrastination	Action	◆》	Progress
#5: Selfishness	◆》	Guilt	Service	◆》	Peace of Mind

DAY 42

Breakfast: Growth is as optional as gratitude.

Lunch: The best has already come and conquered; only gratitude remains.

Dinner: Leadership challenged from obscurity violates gratitude.

Snack: Applied gratitude is more powerful than lonely knowledge.

Misplaced Focus		Negative Result	Redirected Focus		Positive Result
#1: Doubt	◆》	Paralysis	Presence	◆》	Passion
#2: Complacency	◆》	Pain	Engagement	◆》	Positive Expectation
#3 Blame	◆》	Powerlessness/ Problems	Resourcefulness	◆》	Possibilities
#4 Indecision	◆》	Procrastination	Action	◆》	Progress
#5: Selfishness	◆》	Guilt	Service	◆》	Peace of Mind

DAY 43

Breakfast: Rainbows are cool and all, but gratitude is more useful.

Lunch: Life plus bad decisions equals gratitude.

Dinner: How you handle frustrations determines if gratitude was involved.

Snack: Gratitude is the music of the misunderstood.

Misplaced Focus		Negative Result	Redirected Focus		Positive Result
#1: Doubt	→	Paralysis	Presence	→	Passion
#2: Complacency	→	Pain	Engagement	→	Positive Expectation
#3 Blame	→	Powerlessness/ Problems	Resourcefulness	→	Possibilities
#4 Indecision	→	Procrastination	Action	→	Progress
#5: Selfishness	→	Guilt	Service	→	Peace of Mind

DAY 44

Breakfast: Silent treatment is prescribed by gratitude.

Lunch: Creativity and procrastination nourish gratitude.

Dinner: Be so busy being you that nobody even thinks to mention gratitude.

Snack: If you're bored, write a book about gratitude.

Misplaced Focus	Negative Result	Redirected Focus	Positive Result
#1: Doubt	Paralysis	Presence	Passion
#2: Complacency	Pain	Engagement	Positive Expectation
#3 Blame	Powerlessness/ Problems	Resourcefulness	Possibilities
#4 Indecision	Procrastination	Action	Progress
#5: Selfishness	Guilt	Service	Peace of Mind

DAY 45

Breakfast: Reach for the stars, but don't completely abandon gratitude.

Lunch: Unintentional consequences are pure sources of gratitude.

Dinner: Something about long car rides, protein, and gratitude pair together well.

Snack: Going with the flow is such a trap. Piss in the stream and try to explain how gratitude works.

Misplaced Focus		Negative Result	Redirected Focus		Positive Result
#1: Doubt	◆》	Paralysis	Presence	◆》	Passion
#2: Complacency	◆》	Pain	Engagement	◆》	Positive Expectation
#3 Blame	◆》	Powerlessness/ Problems	Resourcefulness	◆》	Possibilities
#4 Indecision	◆》	Procrastination	Action	◆》	Progress
#5: Selfishness	◆》	Guilt	Service	◆》	Peace of Mind

DAY 46

Breakfast: Not knowing is a good thing, start with gratitude.

Lunch: Four different seasons work out a little better with gratitude.

Dinner: The destination of gratitude is known only by those who experience it.

Snack: Hidden gratitude produces rebellious behavior.

Misplaced Focus		Negative Result	Redirected Focus		Positive Result
#1: Doubt	»	Paralysis	Presence	»	Passion
#2: Complacency	»	Pain	Engagement	»	Positive Expectation
#3 Blame	»	Powerlessness/ Problems	Resourcefulness	»	Possibilities
#4 Indecision	»	Procrastination	Action	»	Progress
#5: Selfishness	»	Guilt	Service	»	Peace of Mind

DAY 47

Breakfast: People are basically dying over toilet paper; gratitude is a piece of shit.

Lunch: Don't let your uniqueness be ruined by a bad encounter with gratitude.

Dinner: Nobody can make you do anything; gratitude is proof.

Snack: If nothing changes, gratitude becomes a magic trick.

Misplaced Focus		Negative Result	Redirected Focus		Positive Result
#1: Doubt	◆»	Paralysis	Presence	◆»	Passion
#2: Complacency	◆»	Pain	Engagement	◆»	Positive Expectation
#3 Blame	◆»	Powerlessness/ Problems	Resourcefulness	◆»	Possibilities
#4 Indecision	◆»	Procrastination	Action	◆»	Progress
#5: Selfishness	◆»	Guilt	Service	◆»	Peace of Mind

DAY 48

Breakfast: Gratitude without forgiveness is deception.

Lunch: Forgiveness without gratitude is normal.

Dinner: Gratitude plays a small role in the story of character.

Snack: Some people are so negative gratitude is an excuse.

Misplaced Focus	Negative Result	Redirected Focus	Positive Result
#1: Doubt	Paralysis	Presence	Passion
#2: Complacency	Pain	Engagement	Positive Expectation
#3 Blame	Powerlessness/ Problems	Resourcefulness	Possibilities
#4 Indecision	Procrastination	Action	Progress
#5: Selfishness	Guilt	Service	Peace of Mind

DAY 49

Breakfast: Lack of faith tarnishes gratitude.

Lunch: The switch that operates gratitude is always broken.

Dinner: Gratitude works best with mistakes.

Snack: Pressure isn't needed to live with gratitude.

Misplaced Focus		Negative Result	Redirected Focus		Positive Result
#1: Doubt	◆》	Paralysis	Presence	◆》	Passion
#2: Complacency	◆》	Pain	Engagement	◆》	Positive Expectation
#3 Blame	◆》	Powerlessness/ Problems	Resourcefulness	◆》	Possibilities
#4 Indecision	◆》	Procrastination	Action	◆》	Progress
#5: Selfishness	◆》	Guilt	Service	◆》	Peace of Mind

DAY 50

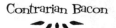

Breakfast: Prove them wrong after you're clear on how gratitude works.

Lunch: Time heals and exposes what gratitude neglects.

Dinner: Don't take things too seriously gratitude—will likely outlive us all.

Snack: Passionate decisions dwarf gratitude.

Misplaced Focus		Negative Result	Redirected Focus		Positive Result
#1: Doubt	◆》	Paralysis	Presence	◆》	Passion
#2: Complacency	◆》	Pain	Engagement	◆》	Positive Expectation
#3 Blame	◆》	Powerlessness/ Problems	Resourcefulness	◆》	Possibilities
#4 Indecision	◆》	Procrastination	Action	◆》	Progress
#5: Selfishness	◆》	Guilt	Service	◆》	Peace of Mind

DAY 51

Breakfast: Without the right amount of gratitude, dreams are exhausting.

Lunch: I have no idea how I got here, but gratitude is trending.

Dinner: Gratitude is preserved through spontaneity.

Snack: Rarely is gratitude mistaken for anything else.

Misplaced Focus		Negative Result	Redirected Focus		Positive Result
#1: Doubt	◆》	Paralysis	Presence	◆》	Passion
#2: Complacency	◆》	Pain	Engagement	◆》	Positive Expectation
#3 Blame	◆》	Powerlessness/ Problems	Resourcefulness	◆》	Possibilities
#4 Indecision	◆》	Procrastination	Action	◆》	Progress
#5: Selfishness	◆》	Guilt	Service	◆》	Peace of Mind

DAY 52

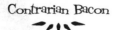

Breakfast: 365 days of gratitude would still be an under sell.

Lunch: The weirdest thing you can do right now is create a résumé and change your name to Gratitude.

Dinner: Debt collectors absolutely love gratitude.

Snack: The craziest thing you can do is claim 100% of your time while practicing gratitude.

Misplaced Focus		Negative Result	Redirected Focus		Positive Result
#1: Doubt	◆》	Paralysis	Presence	◆》	Passion
#2: Complacency	◆》	Pain	Engagement	◆》	Positive Expectation
#3 Blame	◆》	Powerlessness/ Problems	Resourcefulness	◆》	Possibilities
#4 Indecision	◆》	Procrastination	Action	◆》	Progress
#5: Selfishness	◆》	Guilt	Service	◆》	Peace of Mind

DAY 53

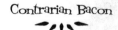

Breakfast: More information related to gratitude can be found at the cemetery.

Lunch: Bad habits learn from gratitude.

Dinner: Thoughts of gratitude crystalize into decisive, loving, and rewarding habits which solidify into circumstances of rightful privilege and appreciation.

Snack: Your life, your decisions, but have you ever heard of gratitude?

Misplaced Focus		Negative Result	Redirected Focus		Positive Result
#1: Doubt	◆》	Paralysis	Presence	◆》	Passion
#2: Complacency	◆》	Pain	Engagement	◆》	Positive Expectation
#3 Blame	◆》	Powerlessness/ Problems	Resourcefulness	◆》	Possibilities
#4 Indecision	◆》	Procrastination	Action	◆》	Progress
#5: Selfishness	◆》	Guilt	Service	◆》	Peace of Mind

DAY 54

Breakfast: If introducing yourself to the world, gratitude is a good place to start and finish.

Lunch: Everyone has their own legitimate agenda; I choose gratitude because I like the price.

Dinner: The definition of gratitude has zero fans.

Snack: Confidence is a roadblock to gratitude.

Misplaced Focus		Negative Result	Redirected Focus		Positive Result
#1: Doubt	◆»	Paralysis	Presence	◆»	Passion
#2: Complacency	◆»	Pain	Engagement	◆»	Positive Expectation
#3 Blame	◆»	Powerlessness/ Problems	Resourcefulness	◆»	Possibilities
#4 Indecision	◆»	Procrastination	Action	◆»	Progress
#5: Selfishness	◆»	Guilt	Service	◆»	Peace of Mind

DAY 55

Breakfast: Gratitude can be independent better than most.

Lunch: Gratitude is packaged in adversity.

Dinner: Some engineering will never be seen or heard of; gratitude operates the same way.

Snack: If gratitude were sold in stores it would be found in the automotive section.

Misplaced Focus		Negative Result	Redirected Focus		Positive Result
#1: Doubt	◆》	Paralysis	Presence	◆》	Passion
#2: Complacency	◆》	Pain	Engagement	◆》	Positive Expectation
#3 Blame	◆》	Powerlessness/ Problems	Resourcefulness	◆》	Possibilities
#4 Indecision	◆》	Procrastination	Action	◆》	Progress
#5: Selfishness	◆》	Guilt	Service	◆》	Peace of Mind

DAY 56

Breakfast: I have to imagine that raising children requires gratitude.

Lunch: Conflict is a friendly reminder from gratitude.

Dinner: When you major in minor things, gratitude has a fighting chance for survival.

Snack: Appearances can be misleading, and gratitude looks quiet.

Misplaced Focus		Negative Result	Redirected Focus		Positive Result
#1: Doubt	◆》	Paralysis	Presence	◆》	Passion
#2: Complacency	◆》	Pain	Engagement	◆》	Positive Expectation
#3 Blame	◆》	Powerlessness/ Problems	Resourcefulness	◆》	Possibilities
#4 Indecision	◆》	Procrastination	Action	◆》	Progress
#5: Selfishness	◆》	Guilt	Service	◆》	Peace of Mind

DAY 57

Breakfast: Without any actors around, stages are still intended for performances of gratitude.

Lunch: Obsession has its place that gratitude allows.

Dinner: At times gratitude is clueless.

Snack: Momentum is sparked by gratitude.

Misplaced Focus		Negative Result	Redirected Focus		Positive Result
#1: Doubt	◆》	Paralysis	Presence	◆》	Passion
#2: Complacency	◆》	Pain	Engagement	◆》	Positive Expectation
#3 Blame	◆》	Powerlessness/ Problems	Resourcefulness	◆》	Possibilities
#4 Indecision	◆》	Procrastination	Action	◆》	Progress
#5: Selfishness	◆》	Guilt	Service	◆》	Peace of Mind

DAY 58

Breakfast: Intolerance ends more relationships than gratitude.

Lunch: Saying yes to gratitude means saying no to skepticism.

Dinner: If you find something worth more than gratitude, @ me—I'm looking too.

Snack: If gratitude had a marketing department, we would all be fired and publicly shamed.

Misplaced Focus		Negative Result	Redirected Focus		Positive Result
#1: Doubt	◆»	Paralysis	Presence	◆»	Passion
#2: Complacency	◆»	Pain	Engagement	◆»	Positive Expectation
#3 Blame	◆»	Powerlessness/ Problems	Resourcefulness	◆»	Possibilities
#4 Indecision	◆»	Procrastination	Action	◆»	Progress
#5: Selfishness	◆»	Guilt	Service	◆»	Peace of Mind

DAY 59

Breakfast: Materialism is the quickest way to misplace gratitude.

Lunch: Refusal to speak life into negativity is my favorite part of gratitude.

Dinner: If reality ever overtakes neutrality, gratitude would be crucified.

Snack: Anybody ready for a National Gratitude Day yet?

Misplaced Focus		Negative Result	Redirected Focus		Positive Result
#1: Doubt	◆》	Paralysis	Presence	◆》	Passion
#2: Complacency	◆》	Pain	Engagement	◆》	Positive Expectation
#3 Blame	◆》	Powerlessness/ Problems	Resourcefulness	◆》	Possibilities
#4 Indecision	◆》	Procrastination	Action	◆》	Progress
#5: Selfishness	◆》	Guilt	Service	◆》	Peace of Mind

DAY 60

Breakfast: Like it or not, you have been profiled several times today thanks to gratitude.

Lunch: People who can't close a sale should shut up and just practice gratitude.

Dinner: Positive thinking is untrained gratitude.

Snack: Banks don't operate on gratitude.

Misplaced Focus		Negative Result	Redirected Focus		Positive Result
#1: Doubt	◆》	Paralysis	Presence	◆》	Passion
#2: Complacency	◆》	Pain	Engagement	◆》	Positive Expectation
#3 Blame	◆》	Powerlessness/ Problems	Resourcefulness	◆》	Possibilities
#4 Indecision	◆》	Procrastination	Action	◆》	Progress
#5: Selfishness	◆》	Guilt	Service	◆》	Peace of Mind

DAY 61

Breakfast: Variety is the thief of gratitude.

Lunch: Resting gives gratitude time to prepare.

Dinner: When nothing makes sense, gratitude is responsible.

Snack: If you make it to day 100 things might get wild; gratitude is weird.

Misplaced Focus		Negative Result	Redirected Focus		Positive Result
#1: Doubt	◆》	Paralysis	Presence	◆》	Passion
#2: Complacency	◆》	Pain	Engagement	◆》	Positive Expectation
#3 Blame	◆》	Powerlessness/ Problems	Resourcefulness	◆》	Possibilities
#4 Indecision	◆》	Procrastination	Action	◆》	Progress
#5: Selfishness	◆》	Guilt	Service	◆》	Peace of Mind

DAY 62

Breakfast: Compounding anything has a payoff, with or without gratitude.

Lunch: Formal lessons are good steppingstones to gratitude.

Dinner: Talent without right use of time complicates gratitude beyond recognition.

Snack: No one is coming to save you—gratitude is your best bet.

Misplaced Focus		Negative Result	Redirected Focus		Positive Result
#1: Doubt	◆》	Paralysis	Presence	◆》	Passion
#2: Complacency	◆》	Pain	Engagement	◆》	Positive Expectation
#3 Blame	◆》	Powerlessness/ Problems	Resourcefulness	◆》	Possibilities
#4 Indecision	◆》	Procrastination	Action	◆》	Progress
#5: Selfishness	◆》	Guilt	Service	◆》	Peace of Mind

DAY 63

Breakfast: Comfort zones are like battlefields for gratitude.

Lunch: The table is set but gratitude is outside participating in a water fight.

Dinner: Looking back at anything distracts the gratitude that was found along the way.

Snack: Good proposals are anchored with gratitude.

Misplaced Focus		Negative Result	Redirected Focus		Positive Result
#1: Doubt	◆》	Paralysis	Presence	◆》	Passion
#2: Complacency	◆》	Pain	Engagement	◆》	Positive Expectation
#3 Blame	◆》	Powerlessness/ Problems	Resourcefulness	◆》	Possibilities
#4 Indecision	◆》	Procrastination	Action	◆》	Progress
#5: Selfishness	◆》	Guilt	Service	◆》	Peace of Mind

DAY 64

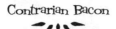

Breakfast: Not often do good intentions end well in my book about gratitude.

Lunch: Those who fight for limitations deserve all the gratitude in the world.

Dinner: Cheating is a form of desperation that despises gratitude.

Snack: Gratitude is evidence that some people do care about humanity.

Misplaced Focus		Negative Result	Redirected Focus		Positive Result
#1: Doubt	◆》	Paralysis	Presence	◆》	Passion
#2: Complacency	◆》	Pain	Engagement	◆》	Positive Expectation
#3 Blame	◆》	Powerlessness/ Problems	Resourcefulness	◆》	Possibilities
#4 Indecision	◆》	Procrastination	Action	◆》	Progress
#5: Selfishness	◆》	Guilt	Service	◆》	Peace of Mind

DAY 65

Breakfast: Minimum effort dominates maximum exposure in the world of gratitude.

Lunch: If money were the only answer, gratitude would have been made popular long ago.

Dinner: Let them ignore you; gratitude sends out cool reminders.

Snack: Actual value perceives gratitude to be useful.

Misplaced Focus		Negative Result	Redirected Focus		Positive Result
#1: Doubt	◆》	Paralysis	Presence	◆》	Passion
#2: Complacency	◆》	Pain	Engagement	◆》	Positive Expectation
#3 Blame	◆》	Powerlessness/ Problems	Resourcefulness	◆》	Possibilities
#4 Indecision	◆》	Procrastination	Action	◆》	Progress
#5: Selfishness	◆》	Guilt	Service	◆》	Peace of Mind

DAY 66

Breakfast: You are your own greatest protection; gratitude is the back-up.

Lunch: At the source of gratitude is mostly awareness.

Dinner: Imagination activates gratitude.

Snack: Each day with gratitude is a day without stress.

Misplaced Focus		Negative Result	Redirected Focus		Positive Result
#1: Doubt	⟫	Paralysis	Presence	⟫	Passion
#2: Complacency	⟫	Pain	Engagement	⟫	Positive Expectation
#3 Blame	⟫	Powerlessness/ Problems	Resourcefulness	⟫	Possibilities
#4 Indecision	⟫	Procrastination	Action	⟫	Progress
#5: Selfishness	⟫	Guilt	Service	⟫	Peace of Mind

DAY 67

Breakfast: After a while pressure becomes gratitude.

Lunch: Mastery is a common starting point for gratitude.

Dinner: Gratitude is the void that consumes fear.

Snack: Never will you hear anyone in their right mind say, "Relax and let gratitude drive."

Misplaced Focus		Negative Result	Redirected Focus		Positive Result
#1: Doubt	◆》	Paralysis	Presence	◆》	Passion
#2: Complacency	◆》	Pain	Engagement	◆》	Positive Expectation
#3 Blame	◆》	Powerlessness/ Problems	Resourcefulness	◆》	Possibilities
#4 Indecision	◆》	Procrastination	Action	◆》	Progress
#5: Selfishness	◆》	Guilt	Service	◆》	Peace of Mind

DAY 68

Breakfast: Use caution: gratitude can be an excellent liar.

Lunch: Irregularity uses gratitude as a weapon.

Dinner: Gratitude is not good or bad until applied to a specific situation.

Snack: The most interesting stories include gratitude.

Misplaced Focus		Negative Result	Redirected Focus		Positive Result
#1: Doubt	◆»	Paralysis	Presence	◆»	Passion
#2: Complacency	◆»	Pain	Engagement	◆»	Positive Expectation
#3 Blame	◆»	Powerlessness/ Problems	Resourcefulness	◆»	Possibilities
#4 Indecision	◆»	Procrastination	Action	◆»	Progress
#5: Selfishness	◆»	Guilt	Service	◆»	Peace of Mind

DAY 69

Breakfast: A great picture taken moments before a catastrophe can sell gratitude as paradise.

Lunch: Work like gratitude does not exist yet and you are a founding member.

Dinner: Debating gratitude limits just about everything.

Snack: Gratitude is the villain of poor representation.

Misplaced Focus		Negative Result	Redirected Focus		Positive Result
#1: Doubt	◆》	Paralysis	Presence	◆》	Passion
#2: Complacency	◆》	Pain	Engagement	◆》	Positive Expectation
#3 Blame	◆》	Powerlessness/ Problems	Resourcefulness	◆》	Possibilities
#4 Indecision	◆》	Procrastination	Action	◆》	Progress
#5: Selfishness	◆》	Guilt	Service	◆》	Peace of Mind

DAY 70

Breakfast: Gratitude won't win many races.

Lunch: Real writers only talk when they get arrested for disturbing the gratitude.

Dinner: Go get a gratitude tattoo and give life all you have.

Snack: Gratitude is a decent emotion.

Misplaced Focus	Negative Result	Redirected Focus	Positive Result
#1: Doubt	Paralysis	Presence	Passion
#2: Complacency	Pain	Engagement	Positive Expectation
#3 Blame	Powerlessness/ Problems	Resourcefulness	Possibilities
#4 Indecision	Procrastination	Action	Progress
#5: Selfishness	Guilt	Service	Peace of Mind

DAY 71

Breakfast: In necessity you will find innovation and echoes of gratitude.

Lunch: Personal titles above all else dilute gratitude.

Dinner: Poised gratitude is not a tradeoff.

Snack: Seeking attention is a waste of gratitude.

Misplaced Focus		Negative Result	Redirected Focus		Positive Result
#1: Doubt	◆》	Paralysis	Presence	◆》	Passion
#2: Complacency	◆》	Pain	Engagement	◆》	Positive Expectation
#3 Blame	◆》	Powerlessness/ Problems	Resourcefulness	◆》	Possibilities
#4 Indecision	◆》	Procrastination	Action	◆》	Progress
#5: Selfishness	◆》	Guilt	Service	◆》	Peace of Mind

DAY 72

Breakfast: Personality shines where gratitude can't reach.

Lunch: Gratitude is sneaky.

Dinner: Freedom is exclusive gratitude to the rescue.

Snack: If you want to quantify gratitude, try yoga and traditional marital sex.

Misplaced Focus	Negative Result	Redirected Focus	Positive Result
#1: Doubt	Paralysis	Presence	Passion
#2: Complacency	Pain	Engagement	Positive Expectation
#3 Blame	Powerlessness/ Problems	Resourcefulness	Possibilities
#4 Indecision	Procrastination	Action	Progress
#5: Selfishness	Guilt	Service	Peace of Mind

DAY 73

Breakfast: Victim mentality is an issue that can't be avoided using gratitude.

Lunch: Bad jokes are hilarious when filtered through gratitude.

Dinner: Worrying helps understand gratitude.

Snack: Enforcement of anything is a threat to everything gratitude symbolizes.

Misplaced Focus		Negative Result	Redirected Focus		Positive Result
#1: Doubt	◆》	Paralysis	Presence	◆》	Passion
#2: Complacency	◆》	Pain	Engagement	◆》	Positive Expectation
#3 Blame	◆》	Powerlessness/ Problems	Resourcefulness	◆》	Possibilities
#4 Indecision	◆》	Procrastination	Action	◆》	Progress
#5: Selfishness	◆》	Guilt	Service	◆》	Peace of Mind

DAY 74

Breakfast: High maintenance is good when gratitude becomes the focus.

Lunch: Hostility is a natural product of gratitude.

Dinner: The ultimate art is gratitude.

Snack: Gratitude allows opportunities to materialize.

Misplaced Focus		Negative Result	Redirected Focus		Positive Result
#1: Doubt	◆»	Paralysis	Presence	◆»	Passion
#2: Complacency	◆»	Pain	Engagement	◆»	Positive Expectation
#3 Blame	◆»	Powerlessness/ Problems	Resourcefulness	◆»	Possibilities
#4 Indecision	◆»	Procrastination	Action	◆»	Progress
#5: Selfishness	◆»	Guilt	Service	◆»	Peace of Mind

DAY 75

Breakfast: Operate from scarcity, live in gratitude.

Lunch: Gratitude is a matrix.

Dinner: Gratitude as a skill depends on circumstances.

Snack: Urgency is crafted with gratitude.

Misplaced Focus		Negative Result	Redirected Focus		Positive Result
#1: Doubt	◆》	Paralysis	Presence	◆》	Passion
#2: Complacency	◆》	Pain	Engagement	◆》	Positive Expectation
#3 Blame	◆》	Powerlessness/ Problems	Resourcefulness	◆》	Possibilities
#4 Indecision	◆》	Procrastination	Action	◆》	Progress
#5: Selfishness	◆》	Guilt	Service	◆》	Peace of Mind

DAY 76

Breakfast: Peace of mind is raw gratitude.

Lunch: Not burning bridges multiplies gratitude.

Dinner: Sizzle sells validation of gratitude.

Snack: Boldness pairs well with gratitude.

Misplaced Focus		Negative Result	Redirected Focus		Positive Result
#1: Doubt	◆》	Paralysis	Presence	◆》	Passion
#2: Complacency	◆》	Pain	Engagement	◆》	Positive Expectation
#3 Blame	◆》	Powerlessness/ Problems	Resourcefulness	◆》	Possibilities
#4 Indecision	◆》	Procrastination	Action	◆》	Progress
#5: Selfishness	◆》	Guilt	Service	◆》	Peace of Mind

DAY 77

Breakfast: Risking gratitude prevents flirting with insanity.

Lunch: Most advice is trash waiting to be collected by gratitude.

Dinner: Waiting is a slippery slope insured by gratitude.

Snack: Change is no accident and gratitude confirms it.

Misplaced Focus		Negative Result	Redirected Focus		Positive Result
#1: Doubt	◆》	Paralysis	Presence	◆》	Passion
#2: Complacency	◆》	Pain	Engagement	◆》	Positive Expectation
#3 Blame	◆》	Powerlessness/ Problems	Resourcefulness	◆》	Possibilities
#4 Indecision	◆》	Procrastination	Action	◆》	Progress
#5: Selfishness	◆》	Guilt	Service	◆》	Peace of Mind

DAY 78

Breakfast: In the world of gratitude, you are where you need to be to experience the most growth for your given circumstance.

Lunch: Approval is not needed for gratitude to take control.

Dinner: Gratitude helps tolerate hindsight.

Snack: Gratitude is a silent fart in a room full of gossip.

Misplaced Focus	Negative Result	Redirected Focus	Positive Result
#1: Doubt	Paralysis	Presence	Passion
#2: Complacency	Pain	Engagement	Positive Expectation
#3 Blame	Powerlessness/ Problems	Resourcefulness	Possibilities
#4 Indecision	Procrastination	Action	Progress
#5: Selfishness	Guilt	Service	Peace of Mind

DAY 79

Breakfast: The trenches show you sides of gratitude that are hard to find anywhere else.

Lunch: Moving on too quickly is not a sign of gratitude.

Dinner: Until you can do it better, do it with gratitude.

Snack: All laws are not written with gratitude because of safety concerns.

Misplaced Focus		Negative Result	Redirected Focus		Positive Result
#1: Doubt	◆》	Paralysis	Presence	◆》	Passion
#2: Complacency	◆》	Pain	Engagement	◆》	Positive Expectation
#3 Blame	◆》	Powerlessness/ Problems	Resourcefulness	◆》	Possibilities
#4 Indecision	◆》	Procrastination	Action	◆》	Progress
#5: Selfishness	◆》	Guilt	Service	◆》	Peace of Mind

DAY 80

Breakfast: If your biggest focus isn't gratitude, welcome to the club.

Lunch: Don't be everything to everybody, be something to somebody dealing in gratitude.

Dinner: Self reflection is a clean source of gratitude.

Snack: The more questions you ask, the less likely gratitude will be the answer.

Misplaced Focus		Negative Result	Redirected Focus		Positive Result
#1: Doubt		Paralysis	Presence		Passion
#2: Complacency		Pain	Engagement		Positive Expectation
#3 Blame		Powerlessness/ Problems	Resourcefulness		Possibilities
#4 Indecision		Procrastination	Action		Progress
#5: Selfishness		Guilt	Service		Peace of Mind

DAY 81

Breakfast: Doing the work looks different for everybody, and gratitude is a convenient equalizer.

Lunch: Without proper guidance, gratitude remains available to access.

Dinner: Instability is a primary function of gratitude.

Snack: In the know is outside the gratitude.

Misplaced Focus		Negative Result	Redirected Focus		Positive Result
#1: Doubt	◆》	Paralysis	Presence	◆》	Passion
#2: Complacency	◆》	Pain	Engagement	◆》	Positive Expectation
#3 Blame	◆》	Powerlessness/ Problems	Resourcefulness	◆》	Possibilities
#4 Indecision	◆》	Procrastination	Action	◆》	Progress
#5: Selfishness	◆》	Guilt	Service	◆》	Peace of Mind

DAY 82

Breakfast: Checking the facts ruins gratitude.

Lunch: Gratitude is a fragment of leadership.

Dinner: Due diligence parties with gratitude.

Snack: Bitterness does not always end at gratitude.

Misplaced Focus		Negative Result	Redirected Focus		Positive Result
#1: Doubt	◆》	Paralysis	Presence	◆》	Passion
#2: Complacency	◆》	Pain	Engagement	◆》	Positive Expectation
#3 Blame	◆》	Powerlessness/ Problems	Resourcefulness	◆》	Possibilities
#4 Indecision	◆》	Procrastination	Action	◆》	Progress
#5: Selfishness	◆》	Guilt	Service	◆》	Peace of Mind

DAY 83

Breakfast: Quality time spent with gratitude wins wars.

Lunch: I have no desire to teach you about gratitude.

Dinner: Gratitude has a reset button known as the opposite sex.

Snack: Transparency locks the doors gratitude already opened.

Misplaced Focus		Negative Result	Redirected Focus		Positive Result
#1: Doubt	◆»	Paralysis	Presence	◆»	Passion
#2: Complacency	◆»	Pain	Engagement	◆»	Positive Expectation
#3 Blame	◆»	Powerlessness/ Problems	Resourcefulness	◆»	Possibilities
#4 Indecision	◆»	Procrastination	Action	◆»	Progress
#5: Selfishness	◆»	Guilt	Service	◆»	Peace of Mind

DAY 84

Breakfast: The sooner you discover your place in the world, the sooner gratitude can prove you wrong.

Lunch: So much energy has gone into bad ideas like gratitude.

Dinner: It isn't difficult to identify who focuses on the benefits that gratitude can provide.

Snack: I would rather be driving but gratitude sold my car.

Misplaced Focus		Negative Result	Redirected Focus		Positive Result
#1: Doubt	◆》	Paralysis	Presence	◆》	Passion
#2: Complacency	◆》	Pain	Engagement	◆》	Positive Expectation
#3 Blame	◆》	Powerlessness/ Problems	Resourcefulness	◆》	Possibilities
#4 Indecision	◆》	Procrastination	Action	◆》	Progress
#5: Selfishness	◆》	Guilt	Service	◆》	Peace of Mind

DAY 85

Breakfast: Like most other things, forcing gratitude won't end well.

Lunch: Nature has the best brand of gratitude.

Dinner: Do it on your own, then do it with gratitude.

Snack: Gratitude was created by pirates.

Misplaced Focus		Negative Result	Redirected Focus		Positive Result
#1: Doubt	◆》	Paralysis	Presence	◆》	Passion
#2: Complacency	◆》	Pain	Engagement	◆》	Positive Expectation
#3 Blame	◆》	Powerlessness/ Problems	Resourcefulness	◆》	Possibilities
#4 Indecision	◆》	Procrastination	Action	◆》	Progress
#5: Selfishness	◆》	Guilt	Service	◆》	Peace of Mind

DAY 86

Breakfast: Closure creates room for gratitude.

Lunch: It has always been the most efficient agenda wins; gratitude won't change that.

Dinner: Gratitude celebrates everything.

Snack: Any process started without gratitude is designed to fail.

Misplaced Focus		Negative Result	Redirected Focus		Positive Result
#1: Doubt	◆»	Paralysis	Presence	◆»	Passion
#2: Complacency	◆»	Pain	Engagement	◆»	Positive Expectation
#3 Blame	◆»	Powerlessness/ Problems	Resourcefulness	◆»	Possibilities
#4 Indecision	◆»	Procrastination	Action	◆»	Progress
#5: Selfishness	◆»	Guilt	Service	◆»	Peace of Mind

DAY 87

Breakfast: From the right angle gratitude looks the same as happiness.

Lunch: Gratitude would have prevented some journeys from happening.

Dinner: Data collected while bypassing gratitude will be misinterpreted.

Snack: Moving targets avoid being stereotyped by gratitude.

Misplaced Focus		Negative Result	Redirected Focus		Positive Result
#1: Doubt	◆》	Paralysis	Presence	◆》	Passion
#2: Complacency	◆》	Pain	Engagement	◆》	Positive Expectation
#3 Blame	◆》	Powerlessness/ Problems	Resourcefulness	◆》	Possibilities
#4 Indecision	◆》	Procrastination	Action	◆》	Progress
#5: Selfishness	◆》	Guilt	Service	◆》	Peace of Mind

DAY 88

Breakfast: Completion means "catch" not finished: Gratitude cheat code #1.

Lunch: If gratitude can't be given freely, it is too expensive.

Dinner: Redundant messaging is reinforcement of gratitude.

Snack: If survival were a group effort, gratitude would be lost.

Misplaced Focus	Negative Result	Redirected Focus	Positive Result
#1: Doubt	Paralysis	Presence	Passion
#2: Complacency	Pain	Engagement	Positive Expectation
#3 Blame	Powerlessness/ Problems	Resourcefulness	Possibilities
#4 Indecision	Procrastination	Action	Progress
#5: Selfishness	Guilt	Service	Peace of Mind

DAY 89

Breakfast: Gratitude can be edited at the expense of flow.

Lunch: Life shifts priorities and gratitude.

Dinner: Being late is a good way to show you understand gratitude.

Snack: First impressions are more important than gratitude to some people.

Misplaced Focus		Negative Result	Redirected Focus		Positive Result
#1: Doubt	»	Paralysis	Presence	»	Passion
#2: Complacency	»	Pain	Engagement	»	Positive Expectation
#3 Blame	»	Powerlessness/ Problems	Resourcefulness	»	Possibilities
#4 Indecision	»	Procrastination	Action	»	Progress
#5: Selfishness	»	Guilt	Service	»	Peace of Mind

DAY 90

Breakfast: Without noise, the signal would lose the benefits of gratitude.

Lunch: Sacrificing the present moment for gratitude is delusional.

Dinner: What is possible always yields to what is necessary regardless of gratitude.

Snack: Gratitude is good for the environment.

Misplaced Focus		Negative Result	Redirected Focus		Positive Result
#1: Doubt	◆》	Paralysis	Presence	◆》	Passion
#2: Complacency	◆》	Pain	Engagement	◆》	Positive Expectation
#3 Blame	◆》	Powerlessness/ Problems	Resourcefulness	◆》	Possibilities
#4 Indecision	◆》	Procrastination	Action	◆》	Progress
#5: Selfishness	◆》	Guilt	Service	◆》	Peace of Mind

DAY 91

Breakfast: Gratitude is a gentle giant with bi-polar tendencies.

Lunch: Open roads lead to gratitude.

Dinner: Immediate responses prove gratitude is a science.

Snack: 3 years from now gratitude will still be gratitude.

Misplaced Focus		Negative Result	Redirected Focus		Positive Result
#1: Doubt	◆》	Paralysis	Presence	◆》	Passion
#2: Complacency	◆》	Pain	Engagement	◆》	Positive Expectation
#3 Blame	◆》	Powerlessness/ Problems	Resourcefulness	◆》	Possibilities
#4 Indecision	◆》	Procrastination	Action	◆》	Progress
#5: Selfishness	◆》	Guilt	Service	◆》	Peace of Mind

DAY 92

Breakfast: Assumptions are rooted in ignorance and monitored by gratitude.

Lunch: More wisdom comes from gratitude than knowledge.

Dinner: Nervousness is excitement lighting fireworks with gratitude.

Snack: Hard to imagine gratitude without camping.

Misplaced Focus		Negative Result	Redirected Focus		Positive Result
#1: Doubt	◆》	Paralysis	Presence	◆》	Passion
#2: Complacency	◆》	Pain	Engagement	◆》	Positive Expectation
#3 Blame	◆》	Powerlessness/ Problems	Resourcefulness	◆》	Possibilities
#4 Indecision	◆》	Procrastination	Action	◆》	Progress
#5: Selfishness	◆》	Guilt	Service	◆》	Peace of Mind

DAY 93

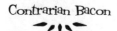

Breakfast: Do the most for the longest amount of time, then blame it on gratitude.

Lunch: People will do anything for fame when gratitude becomes old.

Dinner: A poorly postured vocabulary launches gratitude into play.

Snack: Searching for the right life with the wrong person is textbook gratitude.

Misplaced Focus		Negative Result	Redirected Focus		Positive Result
#1: Doubt	◆》	Paralysis	Presence	◆》	Passion
#2: Complacency	◆》	Pain	Engagement	◆》	Positive Expectation
#3 Blame	◆》	Powerlessness/ Problems	Resourcefulness	◆》	Possibilities
#4 Indecision	◆》	Procrastination	Action	◆》	Progress
#5: Selfishness	◆》	Guilt	Service	◆》	Peace of Mind

DAY 94

Breakfast: Fast transactions rarely involve gratitude.

Lunch: Gratitude is a good strategy for shopping.

Dinner: True gratitude demands that you get very drunk at least once a year.

Snack: Gratitude is an emotional muscle that needs to be trained.

Misplaced Focus		Negative Result	Redirected Focus		Positive Result
#1: Doubt	»	Paralysis	Presence	»	Passion
#2: Complacency	»	Pain	Engagement	»	Positive Expectation
#3 Blame	»	Powerlessness/ Problems	Resourcefulness	»	Possibilities
#4 Indecision	»	Procrastination	Action	»	Progress
#5: Selfishness	»	Guilt	Service	»	Peace of Mind

DAY 95

Breakfast: Paranoia creeps in like gratitude leaks out.

Lunch: Special conditions cloud the judgement of gratitude.

Dinner: The clock moves the same for everyone and gratitude has no favorites.

Snack: Cruelty is a scheme of gratitude.

Misplaced Focus		Negative Result	Redirected Focus		Positive Result
#1: Doubt	»	Paralysis	Presence	»	Passion
#2: Complacency	»	Pain	Engagement	»	Positive Expectation
#3 Blame	»	Powerlessness/ Problems	Resourcefulness	»	Possibilities
#4 Indecision	»	Procrastination	Action	»	Progress
#5: Selfishness	»	Guilt	Service	»	Peace of Mind

DAY 96

Breakfast: Gratitude denies restraint.

Lunch: Charity begins where gratitude ends.

Dinner: Positions of power idolize gratitude.

Snack: Why would you ever borrow gratitude?

Misplaced Focus	Negative Result	Redirected Focus	Positive Result
#1: Doubt	Paralysis	Presence	Passion
#2: Complacency	Pain	Engagement	Positive Expectation
#3 Blame	Powerlessness/ Problems	Resourcefulness	Possibilities
#4 Indecision	Procrastination	Action	Progress
#5: Selfishness	Guilt	Service	Peace of Mind

DAY 97

Breakfast: Inspiration is a cheaper version of gratitude.

Lunch: How dare you not mention gratitude?

Dinner: Don't expect help with issues that can be solved with gratitude.

Snack: Gratitude can only be objectified by the living.

Misplaced Focus		Negative Result	Redirected Focus		Positive Result
#1: Doubt	◆》	Paralysis	Presence	◆》	Passion
#2: Complacency	◆》	Pain	Engagement	◆》	Positive Expectation
#3 Blame	◆》	Powerlessness/ Problems	Resourcefulness	◆》	Possibilities
#4 Indecision	◆》	Procrastination	Action	◆》	Progress
#5: Selfishness	◆》	Guilt	Service	◆》	Peace of Mind

DAY 98

Breakfast: Gratitude is often targeted with forfeiture.

Lunch: Undeserved gratitude is a common experience.

Dinner: The lowest threshold for pain was constructed by gratitude.

Snack: Where is the gratitude emoji?

Misplaced Focus		Negative Result	Redirected Focus		Positive Result
#1: Doubt	◆》	Paralysis	Presence	◆》	Passion
#2: Complacency	◆》	Pain	Engagement	◆》	Positive Expectation
#3 Blame	◆》	Powerlessness/ Problems	Resourcefulness	◆》	Possibilities
#4 Indecision	◆》	Procrastination	Action	◆》	Progress
#5: Selfishness	◆》	Guilt	Service	◆》	Peace of Mind

DAY 99

Breakfast: Science experiments are introductions to Gratitude 101.

Lunch: Exploration is the fun side of gratitude.

Dinner: Gratitude coordinates with certainty.

Snack: Gratitude impairs fear.

Misplaced Focus		Negative Result	Redirected Focus		Positive Result
#1: Doubt	◆》	Paralysis	Presence	◆》	Passion
#2: Complacency	◆》	Pain	Engagement	◆》	Positive Expectation
#3 Blame	◆》	Powerlessness/ Problems	Resourcefulness	◆》	Possibilities
#4 Indecision	◆》	Procrastination	Action	◆》	Progress
#5: Selfishness	◆》	Guilt	Service	◆》	Peace of Mind

DAY 100

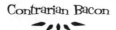

Breakfast: The calmest is either the most foolish or most familiar with gratitude.

Lunch: Gratitude is what you make it.

Dinner: Don't exchange gratitude for convenience.

Snack: To be alive is to know gratitude.

Misplaced Focus		Negative Result	Redirected Focus		Positive Result
#1: Doubt	◆》	Paralysis	Presence	◆》	Passion
#2: Complacency	◆》	Pain	Engagement	◆》	Positive Expectation
#3 Blame	◆》	Powerlessness/ Problems	Resourcefulness	◆》	Possibilities
#4 Indecision	◆》	Procrastination	Action	◆》	Progress
#5: Selfishness	◆》	Guilt	Service	◆》	Peace of Mind

100 Days of Patience

The Contrarian's Solution

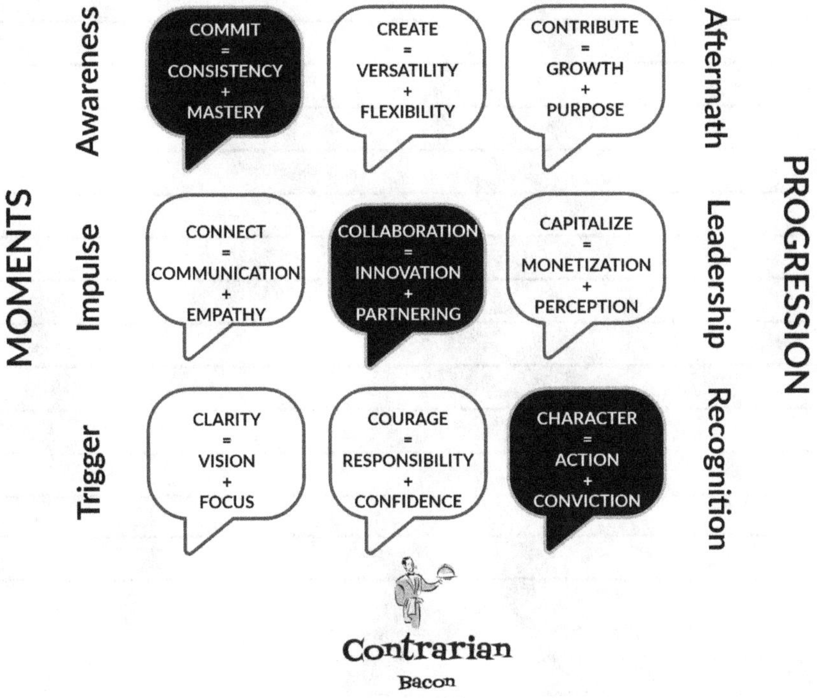

DAY 1

Breakfast: Patience is a powerful habit to develop.

Lunch: Short quotes about patience are genius.

Dinner: Patience has more to do with behavior than time.

Snack: Show me a great accomplishment that discredits patience?

Misplaced Focus		Negative Result	Redirected Focus		Positive Result
#1: Doubt	◆》	Paralysis	Presence	◆》	Passion
#2: Complacency	◆》	Pain	Engagement	◆》	Positive Expectation
#3 Blame	◆》	Powerlessness/ Problems	Resourcefulness	◆》	Possibilities
#4 Indecision	◆》	Procrastination	Action	◆》	Progress
#5: Selfishness	◆》	Guilt	Service	◆》	Peace of Mind

DAY 2

Breakfast: Rushing patience is a bad idea; slow your roll, little nugget.

Lunch: Nothing intensifies patience quite like arrogance.

Dinner: Potential patience is that dream nobody remembers.

Snack: Patience challenges don't really have clear guidelines.

Misplaced Focus		Negative Result	Redirected Focus		Positive Result
#1: Doubt	◆»	Paralysis	Presence	◆»	Passion
#2: Complacency	◆»	Pain	Engagement	◆»	Positive Expectation
#3 Blame	◆»	Powerlessness/ Problems	Resourcefulness	◆»	Possibilities
#4 Indecision	◆»	Procrastination	Action	◆»	Progress
#5: Selfishness	◆»	Guilt	Service	◆»	Peace of Mind

DAY 3

Breakfast: Working full time at anything builds or destroys patience.

Lunch: Proper pouring dances with patience.

Dinner: Imagine jumping off a bridge with no equipment; now use patience and make better decisions please and thank you.

Snack: Pure confidence has small traces of patience.

Misplaced Focus		Negative Result	Redirected Focus		Positive Result
#1: Doubt	◆》	Paralysis	Presence	◆》	Passion
#2: Complacency	◆》	Pain	Engagement	◆》	Positive Expectation
#3 Blame	◆》	Powerlessness/ Problems	Resourcefulness	◆》	Possibilities
#4 Indecision	◆》	Procrastination	Action	◆》	Progress
#5: Selfishness	◆》	Guilt	Service	◆》	Peace of Mind

DAY 4

Breakfast: Patience makes a bunch of mistakes.

Lunch: Don't let patience avoid the risks that help strengthen faith.

Dinner: Duplication is patience inside out.

Snack: Mastery of patience is...

Misplaced Focus		Negative Result	Redirected Focus		Positive Result
#1: Doubt	◆》	Paralysis	Presence	◆》	Passion
#2: Complacency	◆》	Pain	Engagement	◆》	Positive Expectation
#3 Blame	◆》	Powerlessness/ Problems	Resourcefulness	◆》	Possibilities
#4 Indecision	◆》	Procrastination	Action	◆》	Progress
#5: Selfishness	◆》	Guilt	Service	◆》	Peace of Mind

DAY 5

Breakfast: Patience without vision is idleness.

Lunch: Patience has no gender.

Dinner: Patience achieves, and force misleads.

Snack: A patient message won't produce fast results unless patience is incentivized better than the most popular mainstream messaging.

Misplaced Focus		Negative Result	Redirected Focus		Positive Result
#1: Doubt	◆》	Paralysis	Presence	◆》	Passion
#2: Complacency	◆》	Pain	Engagement	◆》	Positive Expectation
#3 Blame	◆》	Powerlessness/ Problems	Resourcefulness	◆》	Possibilities
#4 Indecision	◆》	Procrastination	Action	◆》	Progress
#5: Selfishness	◆》	Guilt	Service	◆》	Peace of Mind

DAY 6

Breakfast: Moving slow is the only thing wrong with patience.

Lunch: Everyone could use a friend who values patience.

Dinner: Keep learning even if patience is everywhere.

Snack: Patience is the woke version of waiting.

Misplaced Focus		Negative Result	Redirected Focus		Positive Result
#1: Doubt	◆》	Paralysis	Presence	◆》	Passion
#2: Complacency	◆》	Pain	Engagement	◆》	Positive Expectation
#3 Blame	◆》	Powerlessness/ Problems	Resourcefulness	◆》	Possibilities
#4 Indecision	◆》	Procrastination	Action	◆》	Progress
#5: Selfishness	◆》	Guilt	Service	◆》	Peace of Mind

DAY 7

Breakfast: When explanations require patience, nobody wins.

Lunch: Use patience as a foundation for personal success.

Dinner: Forward thinking combined with patience
can accomplish almost anything.

Snack: Patience has no bank account.

Misplaced Focus		Negative Result	Redirected Focus		Positive Result
#1: Doubt	◆》	Paralysis	Presence	◆》	Passion
#2: Complacency	◆》	Pain	Engagement	◆》	Positive Expectation
#3 Blame	◆》	Powerlessness/ Problems	Resourcefulness	◆》	Possibilities
#4 Indecision	◆》	Procrastination	Action	◆》	Progress
#5: Selfishness	◆》	Guilt	Service	◆》	Peace of Mind

DAY 8

Breakfast: Missed free throws require patience.

Lunch: Where patience is thinnest, doubt accumulates.

Dinner: Witnessed patience is perpetual.

Snack: Authentic patience should never be discounted.

Misplaced Focus		Negative Result	Redirected Focus		Positive Result
#1: Doubt	◆»	Paralysis	Presence	◆»	Passion
#2: Complacency	◆»	Pain	Engagement	◆»	Positive Expectation
#3 Blame	◆»	Powerlessness/ Problems	Resourcefulness	◆»	Possibilities
#4 Indecision	◆»	Procrastination	Action	◆»	Progress
#5: Selfishness	◆»	Guilt	Service	◆»	Peace of Mind

DAY 9

Breakfast: Good penmanship reflects consistency and patience.

Lunch: Patience experts all agree that you can't actually "win" the lottery.

Dinner: Cages are the consequences of uncontrolled patience.

Snack: To memorize every quote in this book requires patience.

Misplaced Focus		Negative Result	Redirected Focus		Positive Result
#1: Doubt	◆》	Paralysis	Presence	◆》	Passion
#2: Complacency	◆》	Pain	Engagement	◆》	Positive Expectation
#3 Blame	◆》	Powerlessness/ Problems	Resourcefulness	◆》	Possibilities
#4 Indecision	◆》	Procrastination	Action	◆》	Progress
#5: Selfishness	◆》	Guilt	Service	◆》	Peace of Mind

DAY 10

Breakfast: The word of the day is patience.

Lunch: Procrastinate with patience and a regulated sense of humor.

Dinner: Only boring stories glorify patience.

Snack: A Lion can have patience too.

Misplaced Focus		Negative Result	Redirected Focus		Positive Result
#1: Doubt	◆》	Paralysis	Presence	◆》	Passion
#2: Complacency	◆》	Pain	Engagement	◆》	Positive Expectation
#3 Blame	◆》	Powerlessness/ Problems	Resourcefulness	◆》	Possibilities
#4 Indecision	◆》	Procrastination	Action	◆》	Progress
#5: Selfishness	◆》	Guilt	Service	◆》	Peace of Mind

DAY 11

Breakfast: Patience in your twenties can't be trusted.

Lunch: Patience with no limits makes good cartoons.

Dinner: Patience is the original social distancing.

Snack: Leverage is patience in motion.

Misplaced Focus		Negative Result	Redirected Focus		Positive Result
#1: Doubt	◆》	Paralysis	Presence	◆》	Passion
#2: Complacency	◆》	Pain	Engagement	◆》	Positive Expectation
#3 Blame	◆》	Powerlessness/ Problems	Resourcefulness	◆》	Possibilities
#4 Indecision	◆》	Procrastination	Action	◆》	Progress
#5: Selfishness	◆》	Guilt	Service	◆》	Peace of Mind

DAY 12

Breakfast: Healthy companionship resembles patience.

Lunch: Voluntary service is desperation or the ultimate symbol of patience.

Dinner: Misfortune can be cured with guidance and patience.

Snack: Patience does not guarantee honor.

Misplaced Focus		Negative Result	Redirected Focus		Positive Result
#1: Doubt	»	Paralysis	Presence	»	Passion
#2: Complacency	»	Pain	Engagement	»	Positive Expectation
#3 Blame	»	Powerlessness/ Problems	Resourcefulness	»	Possibilities
#4 Indecision	»	Procrastination	Action	»	Progress
#5: Selfishness	»	Guilt	Service	»	Peace of Mind

DAY 13

Breakfast: When the dust settles, patience is the clear winner.

Lunch: Mass approval is not an act of patience.

Dinner: Perspective should be avoided absent of patience.

Snack: Patience that is easily offended is self esteem pretending to not care.

Misplaced Focus		Negative Result	Redirected Focus		Positive Result
#1: Doubt	◆》	Paralysis	Presence	◆》	Passion
#2: Complacency	◆》	Pain	Engagement	◆》	Positive Expectation
#3 Blame	◆》	Powerlessness/ Problems	Resourcefulness	◆》	Possibilities
#4 Indecision	◆》	Procrastination	Action	◆》	Progress
#5: Selfishness	◆》	Guilt	Service	◆》	Peace of Mind

DAY 14

Breakfast: If everybody is saying the same thing about you and it relates to patience, nature smiles and keeps reading.

Lunch: Depth is consumed by patience; don't go if you don't know.

Dinner: Cooperation challenged by patience properly becomes unity.

Snack: Prejudice is the worthy rival of patience.

Misplaced Focus	Negative Result	Redirected Focus	Positive Result
#1: Doubt	Paralysis	Presence	Passion
#2: Complacency	Pain	Engagement	Positive Expectation
#3 Blame	Powerlessness/ Problems	Resourcefulness	Possibilities
#4 Indecision	Procrastination	Action	Progress
#5: Selfishness	Guilt	Service	Peace of Mind

DAY 15

Breakfast: A virus is the weaponization of patience.

Lunch: Effective communication commands patience.

Dinner: The most known solutions are void of patience.

Snack: Confusion is bound by simulations of patience.

Misplaced Focus		Negative Result	Redirected Focus		Positive Result
#1: Doubt	◆»	Paralysis	Presence	◆»	Passion
#2: Complacency	◆»	Pain	Engagement	◆»	Positive Expectation
#3 Blame	◆»	Powerlessness/ Problems	Resourcefulness	◆»	Possibilities
#4 Indecision	◆»	Procrastination	Action	◆»	Progress
#5: Selfishness	◆»	Guilt	Service	◆»	Peace of Mind

DAY 16

Breakfast: Loss of patience is premeditated.

Lunch: Modern patience is disguised as indifference.

Dinner: If everything happened simultaneously, how would patience be identified?

Snack: Overcooking patience is not possible.

Misplaced Focus		Negative Result	Redirected Focus		Positive Result
#1: Doubt	◆》	Paralysis	Presence	◆》	Passion
#2: Complacency	◆》	Pain	Engagement	◆》	Positive Expectation
#3 Blame	◆》	Powerlessness/ Problems	Resourcefulness	◆》	Possibilities
#4 Indecision	◆》	Procrastination	Action	◆》	Progress
#5: Selfishness	◆》	Guilt	Service	◆》	Peace of Mind

DAY 17

Breakfast: Gathering hundreds of untrained kids together is patience, not school.

Lunch: Practicing patience is not a game winning strategy.

Dinner: When patience is the moral of the story, life narrates.

Snack: Patience is a reflection of light.

Misplaced Focus		Negative Result	Redirected Focus		Positive Result
#1: Doubt	◆》	Paralysis	Presence	◆》	Passion
#2: Complacency	◆》	Pain	Engagement	◆》	Positive Expectation
#3 Blame	◆》	Powerlessness/ Problems	Resourcefulness	◆》	Possibilities
#4 Indecision	◆》	Procrastination	Action	◆》	Progress
#5: Selfishness	◆》	Guilt	Service	◆》	Peace of Mind

DAY 18

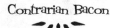

Breakfast: In the most difficult situations, patience takes a snack break.

Lunch: The story of patience is told by drunken silence.

Dinner: Dementia is a spicy version of déjà vu mixed with a hint of patience.

Snack: To some, patience only offers discomfort.

Misplaced Focus		Negative Result	Redirected Focus		Positive Result
#1: Doubt	◆》	Paralysis	Presence	◆》	Passion
#2: Complacency	◆》	Pain	Engagement	◆》	Positive Expectation
#3 Blame	◆》	Powerlessness/ Problems	Resourcefulness	◆》	Possibilities
#4 Indecision	◆》	Procrastination	Action	◆》	Progress
#5: Selfishness	◆》	Guilt	Service	◆》	Peace of Mind

DAY 19

Breakfast: False confidence corrupts true patience in movies.

Lunch: Even if you travel the wrong direction for 365 days, if you meet the right people patience will find you.

Dinner: Overthinking is a negative side effect of too much patience.

Snack: Encouragement thrives off patience.

Misplaced Focus		Negative Result	Redirected Focus		Positive Result
#1: Doubt	◆》	Paralysis	Presence	◆》	Passion
#2: Complacency	◆》	Pain	Engagement	◆》	Positive Expectation
#3 Blame	◆》	Powerlessness/ Problems	Resourcefulness	◆》	Possibilities
#4 Indecision	◆》	Procrastination	Action	◆》	Progress
#5: Selfishness	◆》	Guilt	Service	◆》	Peace of Mind

DAY 20

Breakfast: The difference between resting and relaxing is patience.

Lunch: Adventures that involve patience are buzz kills.

Dinner: Patience creates excellent rules.

Snack: Patience in the future has anxiety.

Misplaced Focus		Negative Result	Redirected Focus		Positive Result
#1: Doubt	◆⟫	Paralysis	Presence	◆⟫	Passion
#2: Complacency	◆⟫	Pain	Engagement	◆⟫	Positive Expectation
#3 Blame	◆⟫	Powerlessness/ Problems	Resourcefulness	◆⟫	Possibilities
#4 Indecision	◆⟫	Procrastination	Action	◆⟫	Progress
#5: Selfishness	◆⟫	Guilt	Service	◆⟫	Peace of Mind

DAY 21

Breakfast: Patience shames imagination.

Lunch: Exploring emotions with patience can help avoid conflict.

Dinner: Negative energy is strangely pulled by patience.

Snack: Recognition of patience ruins everything.

Misplaced Focus		Negative Result	Redirected Focus		Positive Result
#1: Doubt	◆》	Paralysis	Presence	◆》	Passion
#2: Complacency	◆》	Pain	Engagement	◆》	Positive Expectation
#3 Blame	◆》	Powerlessness/ Problems	Resourcefulness	◆》	Possibilities
#4 Indecision	◆》	Procrastination	Action	◆》	Progress
#5: Selfishness	◆》	Guilt	Service	◆》	Peace of Mind

DAY 22

Breakfast: Regarding leadership, patience can be easily mistaken for incompetence.

Lunch: Past successes are more valuable than current successes that disregard patience as a priority.

Dinner: Seeds are the biggest fans of patience.

Snack: If you know what patience is then you know you don't have any.

Misplaced Focus	Negative Result	Redirected Focus	Positive Result
#1: Doubt	Paralysis	Presence	Passion
#2: Complacency	Pain	Engagement	Positive Expectation
#3 Blame	Powerlessness/ Problems	Resourcefulness	Possibilities
#4 Indecision	Procrastination	Action	Progress
#5: Selfishness	Guilt	Service	Peace of Mind

DAY 23

Breakfast: Privatizing, relating to efforts of public patience makes good secrets.

Lunch: Joy found in patience is the gold standard.

Dinner: Never say this aloud, but patience is the only theory worth explaining.

Snack: Doubting patience is commitment to fear.

Misplaced Focus		Negative Result	Redirected Focus		Positive Result
#1: Doubt	◆》	Paralysis	Presence	◆》	Passion
#2: Complacency	◆》	Pain	Engagement	◆》	Positive Expectation
#3 Blame	◆》	Powerlessness/ Problems	Resourcefulness	◆》	Possibilities
#4 Indecision	◆》	Procrastination	Action	◆》	Progress
#5: Selfishness	◆》	Guilt	Service	◆》	Peace of Mind

DAY 24

Breakfast: Authority disturbs the proper function of patience.

Lunch: Patience does not come with certainty.

Dinner: Engaging with patience feels wrong at first.

Snack: Inferiority is accepted when patience is rejected.

Misplaced Focus	Negative Result	Redirected Focus	Positive Result
#1: Doubt	Paralysis	Presence	Passion
#2: Complacency	Pain	Engagement	Positive Expectation
#3 Blame	Powerlessness/ Problems	Resourcefulness	Possibilities
#4 Indecision	Procrastination	Action	Progress
#5: Selfishness	Guilt	Service	Peace of Mind

DAY 25

Breakfast: When decisions seem permanent, patience has defeated you.

Lunch: Becoming anything without patience might not be worth talking about.

Dinner: Sustainability focused efforts require urgency and patience.

Snack: Resentment of trends is a gateway to patience.

Misplaced Focus		Negative Result	Redirected Focus		Positive Result
#1: Doubt	»	Paralysis	Presence	»	Passion
#2: Complacency	»	Pain	Engagement	»	Positive Expectation
#3 Blame	»	Powerlessness/ Problems	Resourcefulness	»	Possibilities
#4 Indecision	»	Procrastination	Action	»	Progress
#5: Selfishness	»	Guilt	Service	»	Peace of Mind

DAY 26

Breakfast: When inward patience is mixed with outward humor, we all win.

Lunch: Extended effort towards work benefits more from endurance than patience.

Dinner: Rumors are sourced from patience.

Snack: Patience is a creative monologue.

Misplaced Focus		Negative Result	Redirected Focus		Positive Result
#1: Doubt	◆》	Paralysis	Presence	◆》	Passion
#2: Complacency	◆》	Pain	Engagement	◆》	Positive Expectation
#3 Blame	◆》	Powerlessness/ Problems	Resourcefulness	◆》	Possibilities
#4 Indecision	◆》	Procrastination	Action	◆》	Progress
#5: Selfishness	◆》	Guilt	Service	◆》	Peace of Mind

DAY 27

Breakfast: Patience is always the villain.

Lunch: Patience is good mental nutrition.

Dinner: Patience is a good excuse to risk it all.

Snack: Real life independence is achieved through patience.

Misplaced Focus		Negative Result	Redirected Focus		Positive Result
#1: Doubt	◆》	Paralysis	Presence	◆》	Passion
#2: Complacency	◆》	Pain	Engagement	◆》	Positive Expectation
#3 Blame	◆》	Powerlessness/ Problems	Resourcefulness	◆》	Possibilities
#4 Indecision	◆》	Procrastination	Action	◆》	Progress
#5: Selfishness	◆》	Guilt	Service	◆》	Peace of Mind

DAY 28

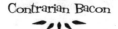

Breakfast: Political gains are like natural disasters that make you question patience and why talking even matters.

Lunch: Separation from unfavorable consequences is maintained by patience and activity.

Dinner: The strings that pull reality are held by patience.

Snack: Originality is born from awkward patience.

Misplaced Focus		Negative Result	Redirected Focus		Positive Result
#1: Doubt	◆》	Paralysis	Presence	◆》	Passion
#2: Complacency	◆》	Pain	Engagement	◆》	Positive Expectation
#3 Blame	◆》	Powerlessness/ Problems	Resourcefulness	◆》	Possibilities
#4 Indecision	◆》	Procrastination	Action	◆》	Progress
#5: Selfishness	◆》	Guilt	Service	◆》	Peace of Mind

DAY 29

Breakfast: Patience does not suggest unlimited.

Lunch: A solid framework includes patience.

Dinner: Liquidity only matters when patience is validated.

Snack: Words are just words, but give me patience and leadership any day.

Misplaced Focus		Negative Result	Redirected Focus		Positive Result
#1: Doubt	◆》	Paralysis	Presence	◆》	Passion
#2: Complacency	◆》	Pain	Engagement	◆》	Positive Expectation
#3 Blame	◆》	Powerlessness/ Problems	Resourcefulness	◆》	Possibilities
#4 Indecision	◆》	Procrastination	Action	◆》	Progress
#5: Selfishness	◆》	Guilt	Service	◆》	Peace of Mind

DAY 30

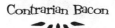

Breakfast: There is a thin line between patience and neglect.

Lunch: Students of patience graduate when they want and how they want.

Dinner: Overnight success is not familiar with patience.

Snack: Breakthroughs are guided by patience and understanding.

Misplaced Focus		Negative Result	Redirected Focus		Positive Result
#1: Doubt	»	Paralysis	Presence	»	Passion
#2: Complacency	»	Pain	Engagement	»	Positive Expectation
#3 Blame	»	Powerlessness/ Problems	Resourcefulness	»	Possibilities
#4 Indecision	»	Procrastination	Action	»	Progress
#5: Selfishness	»	Guilt	Service	»	Peace of Mind

DAY 31

Breakfast: Being afraid to have patience opens the door for failure.

Lunch: Complex scenarios are patience exercises.

Dinner: Answer with patience.

Snack: Patience glows in the dark.

Misplaced Focus		Negative Result	Redirected Focus		Positive Result
#1: Doubt	◆》	Paralysis	Presence	◆》	Passion
#2: Complacency	◆》	Pain	Engagement	◆》	Positive Expectation
#3 Blame	◆》	Powerlessness/ Problems	Resourcefulness	◆》	Possibilities
#4 Indecision	◆》	Procrastination	Action	◆》	Progress
#5: Selfishness	◆》	Guilt	Service	◆》	Peace of Mind

DAY 32

Breakfast: Quitting is the same as hiding from patience.

Lunch: When patience becomes as important as convenience, things will get interesting.

Dinner: Lazy ideas eventually transition to patience.

Snack: Well kept patience is old news.

Misplaced Focus	Negative Result	Redirected Focus	Positive Result
#1: Doubt	Paralysis	Presence	Passion
#2: Complacency	Pain	Engagement	Positive Expectation
#3 Blame	Powerlessness/ Problems	Resourcefulness	Possibilities
#4 Indecision	Procrastination	Action	Progress
#5: Selfishness	Guilt	Service	Peace of Mind

DAY 33

Breakfast: Bravery charges patience monthly rent.

Lunch: If names ring bells, patience is the bell once it returns to the lowest vibration.

Dinner: Indecision is regulated by patience.

Snack: Body language speaks patience.

Misplaced Focus		Negative Result	Redirected Focus		Positive Result
#1: Doubt	◆》	Paralysis	Presence	◆》	Passion
#2: Complacency	◆》	Pain	Engagement	◆》	Positive Expectation
#3 Blame	◆》	Powerlessness/ Problems	Resourcefulness	◆》	Possibilities
#4 Indecision	◆》	Procrastination	Action	◆》	Progress
#5: Selfishness	◆》	Guilt	Service	◆》	Peace of Mind

DAY 34

Breakfast: Distancing caused by patience is priceless.

Lunch: If the smallest step forward is patience, do it while taking a smiling picture.

Dinner: The center of love is a pattern of patience.

Snack: Art says very little without patience.

Misplaced Focus		Negative Result	Redirected Focus		Positive Result
#1: Doubt	◆》	Paralysis	Presence	◆》	Passion
#2: Complacency	◆》	Pain	Engagement	◆》	Positive Expectation
#3 Blame	◆》	Powerlessness/ Problems	Resourcefulness	◆》	Possibilities
#4 Indecision	◆》	Procrastination	Action	◆》	Progress
#5: Selfishness	◆》	Guilt	Service	◆》	Peace of Mind

DAY 35

Breakfast: The heaviest example of patience is doubt.

Lunch: If what would have made you happy is gone, use patience and identify what will make you the happiest.

Dinner: Hopeful patience is just wrong.

Snack: Consistent trouble is patience figuring out what works.

Misplaced Focus		Negative Result	Redirected Focus		Positive Result
#1: Doubt	◆》	Paralysis	Presence	◆》	Passion
#2: Complacency	◆》	Pain	Engagement	◆》	Positive Expectation
#3 Blame	◆》	Powerlessness/ Problems	Resourcefulness	◆》	Possibilities
#4 Indecision	◆》	Procrastination	Action	◆》	Progress
#5: Selfishness	◆》	Guilt	Service	◆》	Peace of Mind

DAY 36

Breakfast: If the village does not value patience, experiment with relocation.

Lunch: High expectations and low patience create nightmares.

Dinner: With patience in rotation, spaces become more enjoyable.

Snack: Difficulties embraced with patience summon triumph.

Misplaced Focus		Negative Result	Redirected Focus		Positive Result
#1: Doubt	»	Paralysis	Presence	»	Passion
#2: Complacency	»	Pain	Engagement	»	Positive Expectation
#3 Blame	»	Powerlessness/ Problems	Resourcefulness	»	Possibilities
#4 Indecision	»	Procrastination	Action	»	Progress
#5: Selfishness	»	Guilt	Service	»	Peace of Mind

DAY 37

Breakfast: To compare patience with anything else takes great skill.

Lunch: Any planet with patience has life.

Dinner: Patience is a slave to circumstance.

Snack: Sincere patience clears the table for real discussion.

Misplaced Focus		Negative Result	Redirected Focus		Positive Result
#1: Doubt	◆》	Paralysis	Presence	◆》	Passion
#2: Complacency	◆》	Pain	Engagement	◆》	Positive Expectation
#3 Blame	◆》	Powerlessness/ Problems	Resourcefulness	◆》	Possibilities
#4 Indecision	◆》	Procrastination	Action	◆》	Progress
#5: Selfishness	◆》	Guilt	Service	◆》	Peace of Mind

DAY 38

Breakfast: Feed the condition that empowers patience.

Lunch: Stretching patience is risky but worth it.

Dinner: Anything blocked because of patience activates curiosity.

Snack: Nature supports patience with fruit.

Misplaced Focus		Negative Result	Redirected Focus		Positive Result
#1: Doubt	◆》	Paralysis	Presence	◆》	Passion
#2: Complacency	◆》	Pain	Engagement	◆》	Positive Expectation
#3 Blame	◆》	Powerlessness/ Problems	Resourcefulness	◆》	Possibilities
#4 Indecision	◆》	Procrastination	Action	◆》	Progress
#5: Selfishness	◆》	Guilt	Service	◆》	Peace of Mind

DAY 39

Breakfast: Don't wish it was easier, wish patience made more sense.

Lunch: Where patience is low, tension is high.

Dinner: If you arrive at patience you've gone too far,
but don't go back. What did you learn?

Snack: The sweetest poem is patience.

Misplaced Focus	Negative Result	Redirected Focus	Positive Result
#1: Doubt	Paralysis	Presence	Passion
#2: Complacency	Pain	Engagement	Positive Expectation
#3 Blame	Powerlessness/ Problems	Resourcefulness	Possibilities
#4 Indecision	Procrastination	Action	Progress
#5: Selfishness	Guilt	Service	Peace of Mind

DAY 40

Breakfast: Rather guess patience than know defeat.

Lunch: Patience is an amazing cheat code.

Dinner: More patience is needed to describe a sentence than a paragraph.

Snack: A loud nation speeds straight past patience.

Misplaced Focus		Negative Result	Redirected Focus		Positive Result
#1: Doubt	◆»	Paralysis	Presence	◆»	Passion
#2: Complacency	◆»	Pain	Engagement	◆»	Positive Expectation
#3 Blame	◆»	Powerlessness/ Problems	Resourcefulness	◆»	Possibilities
#4 Indecision	◆»	Procrastination	Action	◆»	Progress
#5: Selfishness	◆»	Guilt	Service	◆»	Peace of Mind

DAY 41

Breakfast: The middle of broke and paid is patience.

Lunch: Choose a team that moves with patience.

Dinner: A job finished quickly can still leverage patience.

Snack: Running through walls might be fun but shows no patience.

Misplaced Focus		Negative Result	Redirected Focus		Positive Result
#1: Doubt	◆》	Paralysis	Presence	◆》	Passion
#2: Complacency	◆》	Pain	Engagement	◆》	Positive Expectation
#3 Blame	◆》	Powerlessness/ Problems	Resourcefulness	◆》	Possibilities
#4 Indecision	◆》	Procrastination	Action	◆》	Progress
#5: Selfishness	◆》	Guilt	Service	◆》	Peace of Mind

DAY 42

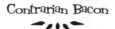

Breakfast: Winter patience and summer patience are not the same.

Lunch: Patience felt in the heart might require a doctor.

Dinner: Perhaps patience is homosexual?

Snack: Patience and colorful reasoning can be phenomenal.

Misplaced Focus		Negative Result	Redirected Focus		Positive Result
#1: Doubt	◆》	Paralysis	Presence	◆》	Passion
#2: Complacency	◆》	Pain	Engagement	◆》	Positive Expectation
#3 Blame	◆》	Powerlessness/ Problems	Resourcefulness	◆》	Possibilities
#4 Indecision	◆》	Procrastination	Action	◆》	Progress
#5: Selfishness	◆》	Guilt	Service	◆》	Peace of Mind

DAY 43

Breakfast: A race engine is built with patience.

Lunch: Remember to reach for patience before excuses.

Dinner: An early grasp of patience illustrates proper guidance.

Snack: Patience is more than using the oven instead of the microwave.

Misplaced Focus		Negative Result	Redirected Focus		Positive Result
#1: Doubt	◆»	Paralysis	Presence	◆»	Passion
#2: Complacency	◆»	Pain	Engagement	◆»	Positive Expectation
#3 Blame	◆»	Powerlessness/ Problems	Resourcefulness	◆»	Possibilities
#4 Indecision	◆»	Procrastination	Action	◆»	Progress
#5: Selfishness	◆»	Guilt	Service	◆»	Peace of Mind

DAY 44

Breakfast: Less money needs more patience.

Lunch: Only patience can diagnose a malfunctioning machine.

Dinner: Signing documents you had no business signing awakens patience.

Snack: Something about patience for a promotion just seems wrong.

Misplaced Focus		Negative Result	Redirected Focus		Positive Result
#1: Doubt	◆》	Paralysis	Presence	◆》	Passion
#2: Complacency	◆》	Pain	Engagement	◆》	Positive Expectation
#3 Blame	◆》	Powerlessness/ Problems	Resourcefulness	◆》	Possibilities
#4 Indecision	◆》	Procrastination	Action	◆》	Progress
#5: Selfishness	◆》	Guilt	Service	◆》	Peace of Mind

DAY 45

Breakfast: For the record, patience ran from slavery too.

Lunch: Absorption leads to saturation of patience.

Dinner: A mile walked with patience can't be logically compared to anything else.

Snack: A positive thought that survives extreme skepticism deserves patience.

Misplaced Focus		Negative Result	Redirected Focus		Positive Result
#1: Doubt	◆》	Paralysis	Presence	◆》	Passion
#2: Complacency	◆》	Pain	Engagement	◆》	Positive Expectation
#3 Blame	◆》	Powerlessness/ Problems	Resourcefulness	◆》	Possibilities
#4 Indecision	◆》	Procrastination	Action	◆》	Progress
#5: Selfishness	◆》	Guilt	Service	◆》	Peace of Mind

DAY 46

Breakfast: Eye had patience in the sun; now writing is fun.

Lunch: Let the haters hate—patience was too expensive.

Dinner: Patience is the study of personal growth.

Snack: Patience matters.

Misplaced Focus		Negative Result	Redirected Focus		Positive Result
#1: Doubt	◆»	Paralysis	Presence	◆»	Passion
#2: Complacency	◆»	Pain	Engagement	◆»	Positive Expectation
#3 Blame	◆»	Powerlessness/ Problems	Resourcefulness	◆»	Possibilities
#4 Indecision	◆»	Procrastination	Action	◆»	Progress
#5: Selfishness	◆»	Guilt	Service	◆»	Peace of Mind

DAY 47

Breakfast: Anything purchased without patience was well marketed.

Lunch: Focus patience on how it is done more than how it is said.

Dinner: In the darkest times patience is the light that asks why.

Snack: What is lost by life is found by patience.

Misplaced Focus		Negative Result	Redirected Focus		Positive Result
#1: Doubt	◆》	Paralysis	Presence	◆》	Passion
#2: Complacency	◆》	Pain	Engagement	◆》	Positive Expectation
#3 Blame	◆》	Powerlessness/ Problems	Resourcefulness	◆》	Possibilities
#4 Indecision	◆》	Procrastination	Action	◆》	Progress
#5: Selfishness	◆》	Guilt	Service	◆》	Peace of Mind

DAY 48

Breakfast: Names help develop patience.

Lunch: If you're in the fire, patience is the enemy.

Dinner: There is a price on your life valued by patience.

Snack: Bad advice creates excellent patience.

Misplaced Focus		Negative Result	Redirected Focus		Positive Result
#1: Doubt	◆》	Paralysis	Presence	◆》	Passion
#2: Complacency	◆》	Pain	Engagement	◆》	Positive Expectation
#3 Blame	◆》	Powerlessness/ Problems	Resourcefulness	◆》	Possibilities
#4 Indecision	◆》	Procrastination	Action	◆》	Progress
#5: Selfishness	◆》	Guilt	Service	◆》	Peace of Mind

DAY 49

Breakfast: Capacity to do anything is outlined with patience.

Lunch: Patience is why quotes are so popular.

Dinner: The legacy of patience is life.

Snack: Identity filtered through patience is enhanced or deteriorated.

Misplaced Focus		Negative Result	Redirected Focus		Positive Result
#1: Doubt	◆》	Paralysis	Presence	◆》	Passion
#2: Complacency	◆》	Pain	Engagement	◆》	Positive Expectation
#3 Blame	◆》	Powerlessness/ Problems	Resourcefulness	◆》	Possibilities
#4 Indecision	◆》	Procrastination	Action	◆》	Progress
#5: Selfishness	◆》	Guilt	Service	◆》	Peace of Mind

DAY 50

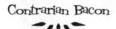

Breakfast: A harmful pattern met with patience neutralizes the aggressor.

Lunch: Most people know how important water is, but patience does not care.

Dinner: Cities have stories, states have patience.

Snack: If control seems hard, having patience should be easy.

Misplaced Focus	Negative Result	Redirected Focus	Positive Result
#1: Doubt	Paralysis	Presence	Passion
#2: Complacency	Pain	Engagement	Positive Expectation
#3 Blame	Powerlessness/ Problems	Resourcefulness	Possibilities
#4 Indecision	Procrastination	Action	Progress
#5: Selfishness	Guilt	Service	Peace of Mind

DAY 51

Breakfast: Patience comes and goes.

Lunch: Commitment that sacrifices patience is weird.

Dinner: The world could be on fire and patience would still wait.

Snack: A one hit wonder must outwork patience.

Misplaced Focus		Negative Result	Redirected Focus		Positive Result
#1: Doubt	◆》	Paralysis	Presence	◆》	Passion
#2: Complacency	◆》	Pain	Engagement	◆》	Positive Expectation
#3 Blame	◆》	Powerlessness/ Problems	Resourcefulness	◆》	Possibilities
#4 Indecision	◆》	Procrastination	Action	◆》	Progress
#5: Selfishness	◆》	Guilt	Service	◆》	Peace of Mind

DAY 52

Breakfast: A slight shift in patience can cause chaos.

Lunch: Saying no to everything somedays is all the patience a smile needs.

Dinner: Everyday gives patience the opportunity to prove why it matters.

Snack: If nothing changes nothing changes, but patience is a decent compromise.

Misplaced Focus		Negative Result	Redirected Focus		Positive Result
#1: Doubt	◆》	Paralysis	Presence	◆》	Passion
#2: Complacency	◆》	Pain	Engagement	◆》	Positive Expectation
#3 Blame	◆》	Powerlessness/ Problems	Resourcefulness	◆》	Possibilities
#4 Indecision	◆》	Procrastination	Action	◆》	Progress
#5: Selfishness	◆》	Guilt	Service	◆》	Peace of Mind

DAY 53

Breakfast: Don't think it can be stressed enough; bring patience to the mirror every time.

Lunch: Ego vs. patience is a good matchup—everyone gets to choose their own winner.

Dinner: Pride sees and hears; soul has patience and listens.

Snack: If patience is your only inheritance, congratulations—you've made it.

Misplaced Focus		Negative Result	Redirected Focus		Positive Result
#1: Doubt	»	Paralysis	Presence	»	Passion
#2: Complacency	»	Pain	Engagement	»	Positive Expectation
#3 Blame	»	Powerlessness/ Problems	Resourcefulness	»	Possibilities
#4 Indecision	»	Procrastination	Action	»	Progress
#5: Selfishness	»	Guilt	Service	»	Peace of Mind

DAY 54

Breakfast: A book that took time gave patience.

Lunch: Doesn't matter if your name comes up—
just about everyone has heard of patience.

Dinner: If patience had a dream, how would we know?

Snack: Inflation is a cute concept waiting to exhale a breath of fresh patience.

Misplaced Focus		Negative Result	Redirected Focus		Positive Result
#1: Doubt	»	Paralysis	Presence	»	Passion
#2: Complacency	»	Pain	Engagement	»	Positive Expectation
#3 Blame	»	Powerlessness/ Problems	Resourcefulness	»	Possibilities
#4 Indecision	»	Procrastination	Action	»	Progress
#5: Selfishness	»	Guilt	Service	»	Peace of Mind

DAY 55

Breakfast: When considering patience, paper or plastic feels so guilty.

Lunch: In flower form patience is eternal.

Dinner: Once patience reaches exhaustion, God will visit us and apologize for all the confusion.

Snack: When you know you don't know; patience is a reminder that knowing anything is flawed.

Misplaced Focus		Negative Result	Redirected Focus		Positive Result
#1: Doubt	»	Paralysis	Presence	»	Passion
#2: Complacency	»	Pain	Engagement	»	Positive Expectation
#3 Blame	»	Powerlessness/ Problems	Resourcefulness	»	Possibilities
#4 Indecision	»	Procrastination	Action	»	Progress
#5: Selfishness	»	Guilt	Service	»	Peace of Mind

DAY 56

Breakfast: If patience wasn't a big deal banks wouldn't need decimals.

Lunch: Why haven't you mastered patience yet?

Dinner: Imagine a business where everyone says no at first but returns with patience.

Snack: Patience patiently waits.

Misplaced Focus		Negative Result	Redirected Focus		Positive Result
#1: Doubt	◆》	Paralysis	Presence	◆》	Passion
#2: Complacency	◆》	Pain	Engagement	◆》	Positive Expectation
#3 Blame	◆》	Powerlessness/ Problems	Resourcefulness	◆》	Possibilities
#4 Indecision	◆》	Procrastination	Action	◆》	Progress
#5: Selfishness	◆》	Guilt	Service	◆》	Peace of Mind

DAY 57

Breakfast: Patience could very well suffer from low self esteem and have us all fooled.

Lunch: Be yourself regardless of trends—it's always time for patience somewhere.

Dinner: Awareness either supports patience or burns it.

Snack: Human history needs patience more than current events.

Misplaced Focus		Negative Result	Redirected Focus		Positive Result
#1: Doubt	◆》	Paralysis	Presence	◆》	Passion
#2: Complacency	◆》	Pain	Engagement	◆》	Positive Expectation
#3 Blame	◆》	Powerlessness/ Problems	Resourcefulness	◆》	Possibilities
#4 Indecision	◆》	Procrastination	Action	◆》	Progress
#5: Selfishness	◆》	Guilt	Service	◆》	Peace of Mind

DAY 58

Breakfast: Patience isn't worth talking about at track meets; all they do is shoot guns and run.

Lunch: Patience is a tool of experience.

Dinner: Whatever can't be done with power is criticized with patience.

Snack: Patience rarely has mass appeal.

Misplaced Focus	Negative Result	Redirected Focus	Positive Result
#1: Doubt	Paralysis	Presence	Passion
#2: Complacency	Pain	Engagement	Positive Expectation
#3 Blame	Powerlessness/ Problems	Resourcefulness	Possibilities
#4 Indecision	Procrastination	Action	Progress
#5: Selfishness	Guilt	Service	Peace of Mind

DAY 59

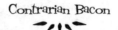

Breakfast: Chances are if there are nine people in a room struggling with patience, you're the tenth.

Lunch: Patience usually isn't the first solution offered.

Dinner: The whole point of racing the clock is blatant disregard for patience.

Snack: Scarcity is real and quality apple juice is worth the patience.

Misplaced Focus		Negative Result	Redirected Focus		Positive Result
#1: Doubt	◆»	Paralysis	Presence	◆»	Passion
#2: Complacency	◆»	Pain	Engagement	◆»	Positive Expectation
#3 Blame	◆»	Powerlessness/ Problems	Resourcefulness	◆»	Possibilities
#4 Indecision	◆»	Procrastination	Action	◆»	Progress
#5: Selfishness	◆»	Guilt	Service	◆»	Peace of Mind

DAY 60

Breakfast: The sharp edge of patience is a pivot point for recklessness.

Lunch: If another word is never spoken, patience to all.

Dinner: Maybe one day I will have the patience to do something worthwhile.

Snack: Don't confuse having patience with not having enough skill.

Misplaced Focus		Negative Result	Redirected Focus		Positive Result
#1: Doubt	◆》	Paralysis	Presence	◆》	Passion
#2: Complacency	◆》	Pain	Engagement	◆》	Positive Expectation
#3 Blame	◆》	Powerlessness/ Problems	Resourcefulness	◆》	Possibilities
#4 Indecision	◆》	Procrastination	Action	◆》	Progress
#5: Selfishness	◆》	Guilt	Service	◆》	Peace of Mind

DAY 61

Breakfast: The best version of yourself has already mastered patience; join the fun.

Lunch: Patience spelled backwards is not a word, keep waiting.

Dinner: Load your gun with patience.

Snack: To get everyone on the same page calls for patience and luck.

Misplaced Focus		Negative Result	Redirected Focus		Positive Result
#1: Doubt	◆》	Paralysis	Presence	◆》	Passion
#2: Complacency	◆》	Pain	Engagement	◆》	Positive Expectation
#3 Blame	◆》	Powerlessness/ Problems	Resourcefulness	◆》	Possibilities
#4 Indecision	◆》	Procrastination	Action	◆》	Progress
#5: Selfishness	◆》	Guilt	Service	◆》	Peace of Mind

DAY 62

Breakfast: Birmingham, Alabama, Patience cheat code #1: 33.518589/-86.810356.

Lunch: Anchorage, Alaska, Patience cheat code #2: 61.216580/-149.899600.

Dinner: Phoenix, Arizona, Patience cheat code #3: 33.448200/-112.072578.

Snack: Little Rock, Arkansas, Patience cheat code #4: 32.715736/-92.289597.

Misplaced Focus		Negative Result	Redirected Focus		Positive Result
#1: Doubt	◆》	Paralysis	Presence	◆》	Passion
#2: Complacency	◆》	Pain	Engagement	◆》	Positive Expectation
#3 Blame	◆》	Powerlessness/ Problems	Resourcefulness	◆》	Possibilities
#4 Indecision	◆》	Procrastination	Action	◆》	Progress
#5: Selfishness	◆》	Guilt	Service	◆》	Peace of Mind

DAY 63

Breakfast: San Diego, California,
Patience cheat code #5: 32.715736/-117.161087.

Lunch: Denver, Colorado, Patience cheat code #6: 39.739235/-104.990250.

Dinner: Connecticut Patience cheat code #7: 41.603222/-73.087746.

Snack: Delaware Patience cheat code #8: 40.301500/-83.067540.

Misplaced Focus		Negative Result	Redirected Focus		Positive Result
#1: Doubt	◆》	Paralysis	Presence	◆》	Passion
#2: Complacency	◆》	Pain	Engagement	◆》	Positive Expectation
#3 Blame	◆》	Powerlessness/ Problems	Resourcefulness	◆》	Possibilities
#4 Indecision	◆》	Procrastination	Action	◆》	Progress
#5: Selfishness	◆》	Guilt	Service	◆》	Peace of Mind

DAY 64

Breakfast: Orlando, Florida, Patience cheat code #9: 28.538336/-81.379234.

Lunch: Atlanta, Georgia, Patience cheat code #10: 33.748997/-84.387985.

Dinner: Hawaii Patience cheat code #11: 19.896767/-155.582779.

Snack: Idaho Patience cheat code #12: 44.068203/-114.742043.

Misplaced Focus		Negative Result	Redirected Focus		Positive Result
#1: Doubt	◆》	Paralysis	Presence	◆》	Passion
#2: Complacency	◆》	Pain	Engagement	◆》	Positive Expectation
#3 Blame	◆》	Powerlessness/ Problems	Resourcefulness	◆》	Possibilities
#4 Indecision	◆》	Procrastination	Action	◆》	Progress
#5: Selfishness	◆》	Guilt	Service	◆》	Peace of Mind

DAY 65

Breakfast: Chicago, Illinois, Patience cheat code #13: 41.883228/-87.632401.

Lunch: Indiana Patience cheat code #14: 40.267193/-86.134903.

Dinner: Iowa Patience cheat code #15: 41.878002/-93097702.

Snack: Kansas Patience cheat code #16: 39.011902/-98.484245.

Misplaced Focus		Negative Result	Redirected Focus		Positive Result
#1: Doubt	◆》	Paralysis	Presence	◆》	Passion
#2: Complacency	◆》	Pain	Engagement	◆》	Positive Expectation
#3 Blame	◆》	Powerlessness/ Problems	Resourcefulness	◆》	Possibilities
#4 Indecision	◆》	Procrastination	Action	◆》	Progress
#5: Selfishness	◆》	Guilt	Service	◆》	Peace of Mind

DAY 66

Breakfast: Kentucky Patience cheat code #17: 37.839333/-84.270020.

Lunch: New Orleans, Louisiana,
Patience cheat code #18: 29.951065/-90.071533.

Dinner: Maine Patience cheat code #19: 45.253784/-69.445473.

Snack: Baltimore, Maryland, Patience cheat code #20: 39.290440/-76.612328.

Misplaced Focus		Negative Result	Redirected Focus		Positive Result
#1: Doubt	◆》	Paralysis	Presence	◆》	Passion
#2: Complacency	◆》	Pain	Engagement	◆》	Positive Expectation
#3 Blame	◆》	Powerlessness/ Problems	Resourcefulness	◆》	Possibilities
#4 Indecision	◆》	Procrastination	Action	◆》	Progress
#5: Selfishness	◆》	Guilt	Service	◆》	Peace of Mind

DAY 67

Breakfast: Boston, Massachusetts,
Patience cheat code #21: 42.358990/-71.058630.

Lunch: Ypsilanti, Michigan, Patience cheat code #22: 42.239811/-83.614540.

Dinner: Minnesota Patience cheat code #23: 46.729553/-94.685898.

Snack: Meridian, Mississippi, Patience cheat code #24: 32.365050/-88.703610.

Misplaced Focus		Negative Result	Redirected Focus		Positive Result
#1: Doubt	◆》	Paralysis	Presence	◆》	Passion
#2: Complacency	◆》	Pain	Engagement	◆》	Positive Expectation
#3 Blame	◆》	Powerlessness/ Problems	Resourcefulness	◆》	Possibilities
#4 Indecision	◆》	Procrastination	Action	◆》	Progress
#5: Selfishness	◆》	Guilt	Service	◆》	Peace of Mind

DAY 68

Breakfast: St. Louis, Missouri, Patience cheat code #25: 38.630280/-60.200310.

Lunch: Montana Patience cheat code #26: 46.879681/-110.362564.

Dinner: Nebraska Patience cheat code #27: 41.492538/-99.901810.

Snack: Las Vegas, Nevada, Patience cheat code #28: 36.169941/-115.139832.

Misplaced Focus		Negative Result	Redirected Focus		Positive Result
#1: Doubt	◆》	Paralysis	Presence	◆》	Passion
#2: Complacency	◆》	Pain	Engagement	◆》	Positive Expectation
#3 Blame	◆》	Powerlessness/ Problems	Resourcefulness	◆》	Possibilities
#4 Indecision	◆》	Procrastination	Action	◆》	Progress
#5: Selfishness	◆》	Guilt	Service	◆》	Peace of Mind

DAY 69

Breakfast: New Hampshire Patience cheat code #29: 43.193851/-71.572395.

Lunch: New Jersey Patience cheat code #30: 40.058323/-74.405663.

Dinner: New Mexico Patience cheat code #31: 34.519939/-105.870087.

Snack: New York Patience cheat code #32: 40.712776-74.005974.

Misplaced Focus		Negative Result	Redirected Focus		Positive Result
#1: Doubt	»	Paralysis	Presence	»	Passion
#2: Complacency	»	Pain	Engagement	»	Positive Expectation
#3 Blame	»	Powerlessness/ Problems	Resourcefulness	»	Possibilities
#4 Indecision	»	Procrastination	Action	»	Progress
#5: Selfishness	»	Guilt	Service	»	Peace of Mind

DAY 70

Breakfast: North Carolina Patience cheat code #33: 35.759575/-79.019302.

Lunch: North Dakota Patience cheat code #34: 47.551495/-101.002014.

Dinner: Cleveland, Ohio, Patience cheat code #35: 41.499321/-81.694359.

Snack: Tulsa, Oklahoma, Patience cheat code #36: 36.155331/-95.992081.

Misplaced Focus	Negative Result	Redirected Focus	Positive Result
#1: Doubt	Paralysis	Presence	Passion
#2: Complacency	Pain	Engagement	Positive Expectation
#3 Blame	Powerlessness/ Problems	Resourcefulness	Possibilities
#4 Indecision	Procrastination	Action	Progress
#5: Selfishness	Guilt	Service	Peace of Mind

DAY 71

Breakfast: Oregon Patience Cheat code #37: 43.804134/-120.554199.

Lunch: Philadelphia, Pennsylvania,
Patience cheat code #38: 39.952583/-75.165222.

Dinner: Rhode Island Patience cheat code #39: 41.580093/-71.477432.

Snack: Myrtle Beach, South Carolina,
Patience cheat code #40: 33.687851/-78.883850.

Misplaced Focus		Negative Result	Redirected Focus		Positive Result
#1: Doubt	◆》	Paralysis	Presence	◆》	Passion
#2: Complacency	◆》	Pain	Engagement	◆》	Positive Expectation
#3 Blame	◆》	Powerlessness/ Problems	Resourcefulness	◆》	Possibilities
#4 Indecision	◆》	Procrastination	Action	◆》	Progress
#5: Selfishness	◆》	Guilt	Service	◆》	Peace of Mind

DAY 72

Breakfast: South Dakota Patience cheat code #41: 43.969517/-99.901810.

Lunch: Nashville, Tennessee, Patience cheat code #42: 36.162663/-86.781601.

Dinner: Houston, Texas, patience cheat code #43: 29.760427/-95.369804.

Snack: Utah Patience cheat code #44: 39.320980/-111.093735.

Misplaced Focus	Negative Result	Redirected Focus	Positive Result
#1: Doubt	Paralysis	Presence	Passion
#2: Complacency	Pain	Engagement	Positive Expectation
#3 Blame	Powerlessness/ Problems	Resourcefulness	Possibilities
#4 Indecision	Procrastination	Action	Progress
#5: Selfishness	Guilt	Service	Peace of Mind

DAY 73

Breakfast: Vermont Patience cheat code #45: 44.558804/-72.577843.

Lunch: Virginia Patience cheat code #46: 37.431572/-78.656891.

Dinner: Washington Patience cheat code #47: 47.751076/-120.740135.

Snack: West Virginia Patience cheat code #48: 38.597626/-80.454903.

Misplaced Focus		Negative Result	Redirected Focus		Positive Result
#1: Doubt	◆》	Paralysis	Presence	◆》	Passion
#2: Complacency	◆》	Pain	Engagement	◆》	Positive Expectation
#3 Blame	◆》	Powerlessness/ Problems	Resourcefulness	◆》	Possibilities
#4 Indecision	◆》	Procrastination	Action	◆》	Progress
#5: Selfishness	◆》	Guilt	Service	◆》	Peace of Mind

DAY 74

Breakfast: Beloit, Wisconsin, Patience cheat code #49: 42.499649/-89.033607.

Lunch: Wyoming Patience cheat code #50: 43.075970/-107.290283.

Dinner: Windsor, Ontario, Patience cheat code #51: 42.314938/-83.036362.

Snack: London, Ontario, Patience cheat code #52: 42.984924/-81.245277.

Misplaced Focus		Negative Result	Redirected Focus		Positive Result
#1: Doubt	◆》	Paralysis	Presence	◆》	Passion
#2: Complacency	◆》	Pain	Engagement	◆》	Positive Expectation
#3 Blame	◆》	Powerlessness/ Problems	Resourcefulness	◆》	Possibilities
#4 Indecision	◆》	Procrastination	Action	◆》	Progress
#5: Selfishness	◆》	Guilt	Service	◆》	Peace of Mind

DAY 75

Breakfast: Toronto, Ontario, Patience cheat code #53: 43.651890/-79.381706.

Lunch: Peru Patience cheat code #54: -9.189967/-75.015152.

Dinner: Angola Patience cheat code #55: -11.202692/17.873886.

Snack: Botswana Patience cheat code #56: -22.328474/24.684866.

Misplaced Focus		Negative Result	Redirected Focus		Positive Result
#1: Doubt	◆》	Paralysis	Presence	◆》	Passion
#2: Complacency	◆》	Pain	Engagement	◆》	Positive Expectation
#3 Blame	◆》	Powerlessness/ Problems	Resourcefulness	◆》	Possibilities
#4 Indecision	◆》	Procrastination	Action	◆》	Progress
#5: Selfishness	◆》	Guilt	Service	◆》	Peace of Mind

DAY 76

Breakfast: Comoros Patience cheat code #57: -11.645500/43.333302.

Lunch: Djibouti Patience cheat code #58: 11.825138/42.590275.

Dinner: Eswatini Patience cheat code #59: -26.326080/31.146080.

Snack: Ghana Patience cheat code #60: 7.946527/-1.023194.

Misplaced Focus		Negative Result	Redirected Focus		Positive Result
#1: Doubt	»	Paralysis	Presence	»	Passion
#2: Complacency	»	Pain	Engagement	»	Positive Expectation
#3 Blame	»	Powerlessness/ Problems	Resourcefulness	»	Possibilities
#4 Indecision	»	Procrastination	Action	»	Progress
#5: Selfishness	»	Guilt	Service	»	Peace of Mind

DAY 77

Breakfast: Ivory Coast Patience cheat code #61: -22.497511/17.015369.

Lunch: Kenya Patience cheat code #62: -0.023559/37.906193.

Dinner: Liberia Patience cheat code #63: 6.428055/-9.429499.

Snack: Morocco Patience cheat code #64: 31.791702/-7.092620.

Misplaced Focus		Negative Result	Redirected Focus		Positive Result
#1: Doubt	◆»	Paralysis	Presence	◆»	Passion
#2: Complacency	◆»	Pain	Engagement	◆»	Positive Expectation
#3 Blame	◆»	Powerlessness/ Problems	Resourcefulness	◆»	Possibilities
#4 Indecision	◆»	Procrastination	Action	◆»	Progress
#5: Selfishness	◆»	Guilt	Service	◆»	Peace of Mind

DAY 78

Breakfast: Namibia Patience cheat code #65: -22.957640/18.490410.

Lunch: Rwanda Patience cheat code #66: -1.940278/29.873888.

Dinner: Sierra Leone Patience cheat code #67: 8.460555/-11.779889.

Snack: Tanzania Patience cheat code # 68: -6.369028/34.888821.

Misplaced Focus		Negative Result	Redirected Focus		Positive Result
#1: Doubt	◆»	Paralysis	Presence	◆»	Passion
#2: Complacency	◆»	Pain	Engagement	◆»	Positive Expectation
#3 Blame	◆»	Powerlessness/ Problems	Resourcefulness	◆»	Possibilities
#4 Indecision	◆»	Procrastination	Action	◆»	Progress
#5: Selfishness	◆»	Guilt	Service	◆»	Peace of Mind

DAY 79

Breakfast: Uganda Patience cheat code #69: 1.373333/32.290276.

Lunch: Zambia Patience cheat code #70: -13.133897/27.849333.

Dinner: Austria Patience cheat code #71: 47.516232/14.550072.

Snack: Bulgaria Patience cheat code #72: 47.733883/25.485830.

Misplaced Focus		Negative Result	Redirected Focus		Positive Result
#1: Doubt	◆》	Paralysis	Presence	◆》	Passion
#2: Complacency	◆》	Pain	Engagement	◆》	Positive Expectation
#3 Blame	◆》	Powerlessness/ Problems	Resourcefulness	◆》	Possibilities
#4 Indecision	◆》	Procrastination	Action	◆》	Progress
#5: Selfishness	◆》	Guilt	Service	◆》	Peace of Mind

DAY 80

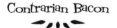

Breakfast: Cyprus Patience cheat code #73: 35.126411/33.429859.

Lunch: Denmark Patience cheat code #74: 56.263920/9.501785.

Dinner: Estonia Patience cheat code #75: 58.595272/25.013607.

Snack: Finland Patience cheat code #76: 61.924110/25.748152.

Misplaced Focus		Negative Result	Redirected Focus		Positive Result
#1: Doubt	◆》	Paralysis	Presence	◆》	Passion
#2: Complacency	◆》	Pain	Engagement	◆》	Positive Expectation
#3 Blame	◆》	Powerlessness/ Problems	Resourcefulness	◆》	Possibilities
#4 Indecision	◆》	Procrastination	Action	◆》	Progress
#5: Selfishness	◆》	Guilt	Service	◆》	Peace of Mind

DAY 81

Breakfast: Georgia Patience cheat code #77: 52.367010/-0.218860.

Lunch: Hungary Patience cheat code #78: 47.162495/19.503304.

Dinner: Ireland Patience cheat code #79: 53.412910/-8.243890.

Snack: Kazakhstan Patience cheat code #80: 48.019573/66.923683.

Misplaced Focus		Negative Result	Redirected Focus		Positive Result
#1: Doubt	◆》	Paralysis	Presence	◆》	Passion
#2: Complacency	◆》	Pain	Engagement	◆》	Positive Expectation
#3 Blame	◆》	Powerlessness/ Problems	Resourcefulness	◆》	Possibilities
#4 Indecision	◆》	Procrastination	Action	◆》	Progress
#5: Selfishness	◆》	Guilt	Service	◆》	Peace of Mind

DAY 82

Breakfast: Lithuania Patience cheat code #81: 55.169437/23.881275.

Lunch: Malta Patience cheat code #82: 35.937496/14.375416.

Dinner: Norway Patience cheat code #83: 60.472023/8.468946.

Snack: Poland Patience cheat code #84: 51.919437/19.145136.

Misplaced Focus		Negative Result	Redirected Focus		Positive Result
#1: Doubt	»	Paralysis	Presence	»	Passion
#2: Complacency	»	Pain	Engagement	»	Positive Expectation
#3 Blame	»	Powerlessness/ Problems	Resourcefulness	»	Possibilities
#4 Indecision	»	Procrastination	Action	»	Progress
#5: Selfishness	»	Guilt	Service	»	Peace of Mind

DAY 83

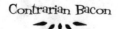

Breakfast: Russia Patience cheat code #85: 61.524010/105.318756.

Lunch: Slovenia Patience cheat code #86: 46.151241/14.995463.

Dinner: United Kingdom Patience cheat code #87: 55.378052/-3.435973.

Snack: Vatican City Patience cheat code #88: 41.902229/12.458100.

Misplaced Focus		Negative Result	Redirected Focus		Positive Result
#1: Doubt	◆》	Paralysis	Presence	◆》	Passion
#2: Complacency	◆》	Pain	Engagement	◆》	Positive Expectation
#3 Blame	◆》	Powerlessness/ Problems	Resourcefulness	◆》	Possibilities
#4 Indecision	◆》	Procrastination	Action	◆》	Progress
#5: Selfishness	◆》	Guilt	Service	◆》	Peace of Mind

DAY 84

Breakfast: Afghanistan Patience cheat code #89: 33.939110/67.709953.

Lunch: Bhutan Patience cheat code #90: 27.514162/90.433601.

Dinner: China Patience cheat code #91: 35.891660/104.195396.

Snack: Israel Patience cheat code #92: 31.046051/34.851612.

Misplaced Focus		Negative Result	Redirected Focus		Positive Result
#1: Doubt	◆》	Paralysis	Presence	◆》	Passion
#2: Complacency	◆》	Pain	Engagement	◆》	Positive Expectation
#3 Blame	◆》	Powerlessness/ Problems	Resourcefulness	◆》	Possibilities
#4 Indecision	◆》	Procrastination	Action	◆》	Progress
#5: Selfishness	◆》	Guilt	Service	◆》	Peace of Mind

DAY 85

Breakfast: Japan Patience cheat code #93: 36.204823/138.252930.

Lunch: North Korea Patience cheat code #94: 40.339851/127.510094.

Dinner: Kuwait Patience cheat code #95: 29.311661/47.481766.

Snack: Lebanon Patience cheat code #96: 33.854721/35.862286.

Misplaced Focus		Negative Result	Redirected Focus		Positive Result
#1: Doubt	◆》	Paralysis	Presence	◆》	Passion
#2: Complacency	◆》	Pain	Engagement	◆》	Positive Expectation
#3 Blame	◆》	Powerlessness/ Problems	Resourcefulness	◆》	Possibilities
#4 Indecision	◆》	Procrastination	Action	◆》	Progress
#5: Selfishness	◆》	Guilt	Service	◆》	Peace of Mind

DAY 86

Breakfast: Mongolia Patience cheat code #97: 46.862495/103.846657.

Lunch: Nepal Patience cheat code #98: 28.394857/84.124008.

Dinner: Oman Patience cheat code #99: 21.473534/55.975414.

Snack: Philippines Patience cheat code #100: 12.879721/121.774017.

Misplaced Focus		Negative Result	Redirected Focus		Positive Result
#1: Doubt	◆》	Paralysis	Presence	◆》	Passion
#2: Complacency	◆》	Pain	Engagement	◆》	Positive Expectation
#3 Blame	◆》	Powerlessness/ Problems	Resourcefulness	◆》	Possibilities
#4 Indecision	◆》	Procrastination	Action	◆》	Progress
#5: Selfishness	◆》	Guilt	Service	◆》	Peace of Mind

DAY 87

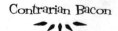

Breakfast: Qatar Patience cheat code #101: 25.354826/51.183884.

Lunch: Sri Lanka Patience cheat code #102: 7.873054/80.721797.

Dinner: Turkey Patience cheat code #103: 38.963745/35.243320.

Snack: United Arab Emirates Patience cheat code #104: 23.424076/53.847816.

Misplaced Focus		Negative Result	Redirected Focus		Positive Result
#1: Doubt	⟫	Paralysis	Presence	⟫	Passion
#2: Complacency	⟫	Pain	Engagement	⟫	Positive Expectation
#3 Blame	⟫	Powerlessness/ Problems	Resourcefulness	⟫	Possibilities
#4 Indecision	⟫	Procrastination	Action	⟫	Progress
#5: Selfishness	⟫	Guilt	Service	⟫	Peace of Mind

DAY 88

Breakfast: Uzbekistan Patience cheat code #105: 41.37749/64.585258.

Lunch: Vietnam Patience cheat code #106: 14.088324/108.277199.

Dinner: Yemen Patience cheat code #107: 15.552727/48.516388.

Snack: Taiwan Patience cheat code #108: 23.697809/120.960518.

Misplaced Focus		Negative Result	Redirected Focus		Positive Result
#1: Doubt	◆》	Paralysis	Presence	◆》	Passion
#2: Complacency	◆》	Pain	Engagement	◆》	Positive Expectation
#3 Blame	◆》	Powerlessness/ Problems	Resourcefulness	◆》	Possibilities
#4 Indecision	◆》	Procrastination	Action	◆》	Progress
#5: Selfishness	◆》	Guilt	Service	◆》	Peace of Mind

DAY 89

Breakfast: Artsakh Patience cheat code #109: 42.369659/-71.158333.

Lunch: Christmas Island Patience cheat code #110: -10.447525/105.690453.

Dinner: Hong Kong Patience cheat code #111: 22.396427/114.109497.

Snack: Sydney Patience cheat code #112: -33.868820/151.209290.

Misplaced Focus		Negative Result	Redirected Focus		Positive Result
#1: Doubt	◆》	Paralysis	Presence	◆》	Passion
#2: Complacency	◆》	Pain	Engagement	◆》	Positive Expectation
#3 Blame	◆》	Powerlessness/ Problems	Resourcefulness	◆》	Possibilities
#4 Indecision	◆》	Procrastination	Action	◆》	Progress
#5: Selfishness	◆》	Guilt	Service	◆》	Peace of Mind

DAY 90

Breakfast: Antarctica Patience cheat code #113: -82.862755/135.000000.

Lunch: Alabama International Dragway
Patience cheat code #114: 34.650630/-87.772640.

Dinner: Alaska Raceway Park Patience cheat code #115: 40.335040/-74.349750.

Snack: Atco Dragway Patience cheat code #116: 39.767899/-74.892342.

Misplaced Focus		Negative Result	Redirected Focus		Positive Result
#1: Doubt	◆》	Paralysis	Presence	◆》	Passion
#2: Complacency	◆》	Pain	Engagement	◆》	Positive Expectation
#3 Blame	◆》	Powerlessness/ Problems	Resourcefulness	◆》	Possibilities
#4 Indecision	◆》	Procrastination	Action	◆》	Progress
#5: Selfishness	◆》	Guilt	Service	◆》	Peace of Mind

DAY 91

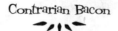

Breakfast: Alabama Dragway Patience cheat code #117: 33.748550/-84.391502.

Lunch: Bandimere Speedway Patience cheat code #118: 39.787239/-86.251953.

Dinner: Bradenton Motorsports Park
Patience cheat code #119: 21.416930/-82.581940.

Snack: Brainerd International Raceway
Patience cheat code #120: 45.594810/-122.694760.

Misplaced Focus		Negative Result	Redirected Focus		Positive Result
#1: Doubt	◆》	Paralysis	Presence	◆》	Passion
#2: Complacency	◆》	Pain	Engagement	◆》	Positive Expectation
#3 Blame	◆》	Powerlessness/ Problems	Resourcefulness	◆》	Possibilities
#4 Indecision	◆》	Procrastination	Action	◆》	Progress
#5: Selfishness	◆》	Guilt	Service	◆》	Peace of Mind

DAY 92

Breakfast: Bristol Dragway Patience cheat code #121: 36.615100/-82.172290.

Lunch: Bunker Hill Drag Strip Patience cheat code #122: 39.314710/-78.048500.

Dinner: Byron Dragway Patience cheat code #123: 52.388450/0.98500.

Snack: Gainesville Raceway Patience cheat code #124: 29.651980/-82.325020.

Misplaced Focus		Negative Result	Redirected Focus		Positive Result
#1: Doubt	◆》	Paralysis	Presence	◆》	Passion
#2: Complacency	◆》	Pain	Engagement	◆》	Positive Expectation
#3 Blame	◆》	Powerlessness/ Problems	Resourcefulness	◆》	Possibilities
#4 Indecision	◆》	Procrastination	Action	◆》	Progress
#5: Selfishness	◆》	Guilt	Service	◆》	Peace of Mind

DAY 93

Breakfast: GALOT Motorsports Park Patience cheat code #125: 39.242730/-77.974730.

Lunch: Great Lakes Dragway Patience cheat code #126: 42.309870/-87.826720.

Dinner: Heartland Motorsports Park Patience cheat code #127: 38.932518/-95.678368.

Snack: Houston Raceway Park Patience cheat code #128: 40.335040/-74.349750.

Misplaced Focus		Negative Result	Redirected Focus		Positive Result
#1: Doubt	◆》	Paralysis	Presence	◆》	Passion
#2: Complacency	◆》	Pain	Engagement	◆》	Positive Expectation
#3 Blame	◆》	Powerlessness/ Problems	Resourcefulness	◆》	Possibilities
#4 Indecision	◆》	Procrastination	Action	◆》	Progress
#5: Selfishness	◆》	Guilt	Service	◆》	Peace of Mind

DAY 94

Breakfast: Las Vegas Nevada Patience cheat code #129: 36.272285/-115.010277.

Lunch: Lucas Oil Raceway Patience cheat code #130: 39.815140/-86.341637.

Dinner: Maple Grove Raceway
Patience cheat code #131: 40.212140/-75.961010.

Snack: Milan Dragway Patience cheat code #132: 42.0821520/-83.682230.

Misplaced Focus		Negative Result	Redirected Focus		Positive Result
#1: Doubt	◆》	Paralysis	Presence	◆》	Passion
#2: Complacency	◆》	Pain	Engagement	◆》	Positive Expectation
#3 Blame	◆》	Powerlessness/ Problems	Resourcefulness	◆》	Possibilities
#4 Indecision	◆》	Procrastination	Action	◆》	Progress
#5: Selfishness	◆》	Guilt	Service	◆》	Peace of Mind

DAY 95

Breakfast: National Trail Raceway

Patience cheat code #133: -35.258770/149.048180.

Lunch: New England Dragway

Patience cheat code #134: 43.019550/-71.028850.

Dinner: Pacific Raceways Patience cheat code #135: 38.484100/-90.741400.

Snack: Palm Beach International Raceway

Patience cheat code #136: 26.688900/-80.084663.

Misplaced Focus		Negative Result	Redirected Focus		Positive Result
#1: Doubt		Paralysis	Presence		Passion
#2: Complacency		Pain	Engagement		Positive Expectation
#3 Blame		Powerlessness/ Problems	Resourcefulness		Possibilities
#4 Indecision		Procrastination	Action		Progress
#5: Selfishness		Guilt	Service		Peace of Mind

DAY 96

Breakfast: Rockingham Dragway
Patience cheat code #137: 43.019550/-71.028850.

Lunch: Route 66 Raceway Patience cheat code #138: 38.654780/-90.133940.

Dinner: Sonoma Raceway Patience cheat code #139: 38.291962/-122.458060.

Snack: Summit Motorsports Park
Patience cheat code #140: 39.241322/-77.975693.

Misplaced Focus		Negative Result	Redirected Focus		Positive Result
#1: Doubt	◆》	Paralysis	Presence	◆》	Passion
#2: Complacency	◆》	Pain	Engagement	◆》	Positive Expectation
#3 Blame	◆》	Powerlessness/ Problems	Resourcefulness	◆》	Possibilities
#4 Indecision	◆》	Procrastination	Action	◆》	Progress
#5: Selfishness	◆》	Guilt	Service	◆》	Peace of Mind

DAY 97

Breakfast: Texas Motorplex Patience cheat code #141: -28.855350/151.165510.

Lunch: Virginia Motorsports Park
Patience cheat code #142: 39.242730/-77.974730.

Dinner: Wild Horse Motorsports Park
Patience cheat code #143: 44.725760/-93.455960.

Snack: Wisconsin International Raceway
Patience cheat code #144: 45.594810/-122.694763.

Misplaced Focus		Negative Result	Redirected Focus		Positive Result
#1: Doubt	◆》	Paralysis	Presence	◆》	Passion
#2: Complacency	◆》	Pain	Engagement	◆》	Positive Expectation
#3 Blame	◆》	Powerlessness/ Problems	Resourcefulness	◆》	Possibilities
#4 Indecision	◆》	Procrastination	Action	◆》	Progress
#5: Selfishness	◆》	Guilt	Service	◆》	Peace of Mind

DAY 98

Breakfast: Woodburn Dragstrip
Patience cheat code #145: 45.148080/-122.860090.

Lunch: Worldwide Technology Raceway At Gateway
Patience cheat code #146: 38.538760/-121.714330.

Dinner: zMAX Dragway Patience cheat code #147: 30.527000/-91.388120.

Snack: Anderson Speedway Patience cheat code #148: 34.512030/-82.593470.

Misplaced Focus	Negative Result	Redirected Focus	Positive Result
#1: Doubt	Paralysis	Presence	Passion
#2: Complacency	Pain	Engagement	Positive Expectation
#3 Blame	Powerlessness/ Problems	Resourcefulness	Possibilities
#4 Indecision	Procrastination	Action	Progress
#5: Selfishness	Guilt	Service	Peace of Mind

DAY 99

Breakfast: Auto Club Speedway Patience cheat code #149: 25.547029/-103.472542.

Lunch: Daytona International Speedway
Patience cheat code #150: 29.075951/-81.246719.

Dinner: Indianapolis Motor Speedway
Patience cheat code #151: 34.072510/-117.566162.

Snack: Michigan International Speedway
Patience cheat code #152: 42.067581/-84.237038.

Misplaced Focus		Negative Result	Redirected Focus		Positive Result
#1: Doubt	◆》	Paralysis	Presence	◆》	Passion
#2: Complacency	◆》	Pain	Engagement	◆》	Positive Expectation
#3 Blame	◆》	Powerlessness/ Problems	Resourcefulness	◆》	Possibilities
#4 Indecision	◆》	Procrastination	Action	◆》	Progress
#5: Selfishness	◆》	Guilt	Service	◆》	Peace of Mind

DAY 100

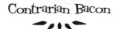

Breakfast: Atlanta Motor Speedway
Patience cheat code #153: 34.072510/-117.566162.

Lunch: Darlington Raceway Patience cheat code #154: 53.224880/-2.953290.

Dinner: Nashville Super Speedway
Patience cheat code #155: 36.045690/-86.403200.

Snack: Milwaukee Mile Patience cheat code #156: 39.721420/-104.952180.

Misplaced Focus	Negative Result	Redirected Focus	Positive Result
#1: Doubt	Paralysis	Presence	Passion
#2: Complacency	Pain	Engagement	Positive Expectation
#3 Blame	Powerlessness/ Problems	Resourcefulness	Possibilities
#4 Indecision	Procrastination	Action	Progress
#5: Selfishness	Guilt	Service	Peace of Mind

100 Days of Preparation

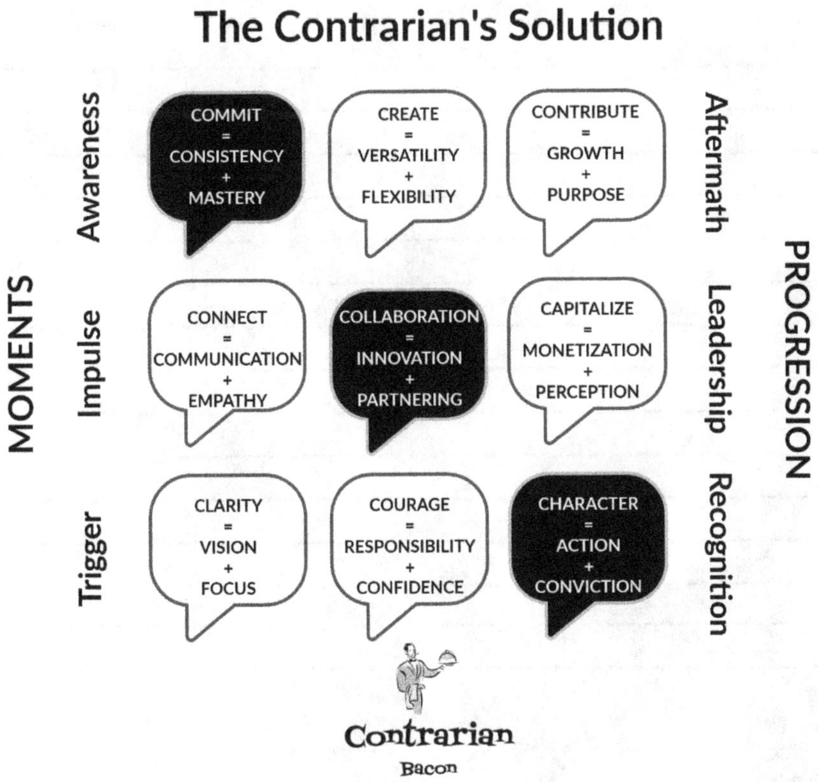

DAY 1

Breakfast: Premature preparation is cool.

Lunch: Proper preparation changes everything.

Dinner: Preparation of excuses serves no purpose.

Snack: Time spent in preparation is sacred.

Misplaced Focus		Negative Result	Redirected Focus		Positive Result
#1: Doubt	◆»	Paralysis	Presence	◆»	Passion
#2: Complacency	◆»	Pain	Engagement	◆»	Positive Expectation
#3 Blame	◆»	Powerlessness/ Problems	Resourcefulness	◆»	Possibilities
#4 Indecision	◆»	Procrastination	Action	◆»	Progress
#5: Selfishness	◆»	Guilt	Service	◆»	Peace of Mind

DAY 2

Breakfast: If preparation isn't absolute after defeat, go home.

Lunch: Preparation determines operation.

Dinner: Accidental preparation is better than procrastination.

Snack: A career without preparation is a trap.

Misplaced Focus		Negative Result	Redirected Focus		Positive Result
#1: Doubt	◆》	Paralysis	Presence	◆》	Passion
#2: Complacency	◆》	Pain	Engagement	◆》	Positive Expectation
#3 Blame	◆》	Powerlessness/ Problems	Resourcefulness	◆》	Possibilities
#4 Indecision	◆》	Procrastination	Action	◆》	Progress
#5: Selfishness	◆》	Guilt	Service	◆》	Peace of Mind

DAY 3

Breakfast: The agenda of preparation is to succeed.

Lunch: If they don't agree with the preparation then the results won't matter.

Dinner: When preparation is secondary, blame is primary.

Snack: Attraction is surrounded by preparation.

Misplaced Focus		Negative Result	Redirected Focus		Positive Result
#1: Doubt	◆》	Paralysis	Presence	◆》	Passion
#2: Complacency	◆》	Pain	Engagement	◆》	Positive Expectation
#3 Blame	◆》	Powerlessness/ Problems	Resourcefulness	◆》	Possibilities
#4 Indecision	◆》	Procrastination	Action	◆》	Progress
#5: Selfishness	◆》	Guilt	Service	◆》	Peace of Mind

DAY 4

Breakfast: If the audience senses lack of preparation, they boo.

Lunch: Groups that don't value preparation can avoid failure masterfully.

Dinner: Preparation applies consistent pressure on leaders.

Snack: The only barrier to preparation is mindset.

Misplaced Focus		Negative Result	Redirected Focus		Positive Result
#1: Doubt	◆》	Paralysis	Presence	◆》	Passion
#2: Complacency	◆》	Pain	Engagement	◆》	Positive Expectation
#3 Blame	◆》	Powerlessness/ Problems	Resourcefulness	◆》	Possibilities
#4 Indecision	◆》	Procrastination	Action	◆》	Progress
#5: Selfishness	◆》	Guilt	Service	◆》	Peace of Mind

DAY 5

Breakfast: Millions require concentration, billions demand preparation.

Lunch: Plateaus approached with preparation are brief advantages.

Dinner: One doesn't enter the Lion's den because of perfect preparation.

Snack: Celebration without preparation is risky business.

Misplaced Focus		Negative Result	Redirected Focus		Positive Result
#1: Doubt	◆》	Paralysis	Presence	◆》	Passion
#2: Complacency	◆》	Pain	Engagement	◆》	Positive Expectation
#3 Blame	◆》	Powerlessness/ Problems	Resourcefulness	◆》	Possibilities
#4 Indecision	◆》	Procrastination	Action	◆》	Progress
#5: Selfishness	◆》	Guilt	Service	◆》	Peace of Mind

DAY 6

Breakfast: Preparation in darkness is less dangerous.

Lunch: The economy is always on the edge of preparation.

Dinner: The amount of preparation necessary to not only taste success but live with it is insane.

Snack: Fairness is an island under attack by preparation.

Misplaced Focus		Negative Result	Redirected Focus		Positive Result
#1: Doubt	◆》	Paralysis	Presence	◆》	Passion
#2: Complacency	◆》	Pain	Engagement	◆》	Positive Expectation
#3 Blame	◆》	Powerlessness/ Problems	Resourcefulness	◆》	Possibilities
#4 Indecision	◆》	Procrastination	Action	◆》	Progress
#5: Selfishness	◆》	Guilt	Service	◆》	Peace of Mind

DAY 7

Breakfast: A generation can be defined by preparation.

Lunch: If you're on the ropes, preparation is in the crowd cheering for your opponent.

Dinner: The ghosts of preparation haunt the regretful.

Snack: A preparation process that gradually becomes more fun is victory.

Misplaced Focus		Negative Result	Redirected Focus		Positive Result
#1: Doubt	◆》	Paralysis	Presence	◆》	Passion
#2: Complacency	◆》	Pain	Engagement	◆》	Positive Expectation
#3 Blame	◆》	Powerlessness/ Problems	Resourcefulness	◆》	Possibilities
#4 Indecision	◆》	Procrastination	Action	◆》	Progress
#5: Selfishness	◆》	Guilt	Service	◆》	Peace of Mind

DAY 8

Breakfast: Equal preparation is a healthy headline for a rivalry.

Lunch: It should be illegal to ignore preparation.

Dinner: The best preparation is confused with hesitation.

Snack: Judgement is poor preparation.

Misplaced Focus		Negative Result	Redirected Focus		Positive Result
#1: Doubt	»	Paralysis	Presence	»	Passion
#2: Complacency	»	Pain	Engagement	»	Positive Expectation
#3 Blame	»	Powerlessness/ Problems	Resourcefulness	»	Possibilities
#4 Indecision	»	Procrastination	Action	»	Progress
#5: Selfishness	»	Guilt	Service	»	Peace of Mind

DAY 9

Breakfast: Holidays are known for kitchen preparation.

Lunch: Late preparation sacrifices potency for clarity.

Dinner: Heavy lifting paired with preparation perpetuates competition.

Snack: Marriage vows symbolize mental preparation.

Misplaced Focus		Negative Result	Redirected Focus		Positive Result
#1: Doubt	◆》	Paralysis	Presence	◆》	Passion
#2: Complacency	◆》	Pain	Engagement	◆》	Positive Expectation
#3 Blame	◆》	Powerlessness/ Problems	Resourcefulness	◆》	Possibilities
#4 Indecision	◆》	Procrastination	Action	◆》	Progress
#5: Selfishness	◆》	Guilt	Service	◆》	Peace of Mind

DAY 10

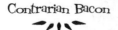

Breakfast: Preparation without internalized motivation is an upset waiting to happen.

Lunch: Preparation exposes miracles.

Dinner: Natural preparation scares me.

Snack: Obligations created by preparation obviously didn't get the message.

Misplaced Focus		Negative Result	Redirected Focus		Positive Result
#1: Doubt	◆》	Paralysis	Presence	◆》	Passion
#2: Complacency	◆》	Pain	Engagement	◆》	Positive Expectation
#3 Blame	◆》	Powerlessness/ Problems	Resourcefulness	◆》	Possibilities
#4 Indecision	◆》	Procrastination	Action	◆》	Progress
#5: Selfishness	◆》	Guilt	Service	◆》	Peace of Mind

DAY 11

Breakfast: Always on indicates no time for preparation.

Lunch: Quiet preparation always evens the odds.

Dinner: Preparation is silly, it's all about practice.

Snack: Preparation is another way to say "always working."

Misplaced Focus		Negative Result	Redirected Focus		Positive Result
#1: Doubt	◆》	Paralysis	Presence	◆》	Passion
#2: Complacency	◆》	Pain	Engagement	◆》	Positive Expectation
#3 Blame	◆》	Powerlessness/ Problems	Resourcefulness	◆》	Possibilities
#4 Indecision	◆》	Procrastination	Action	◆》	Progress
#5: Selfishness	◆》	Guilt	Service	◆》	Peace of Mind

DAY 12

Breakfast: Biggest difference between the pole and a poll is preparation.

Lunch: Purposeful preparation is a personal relationship.

Dinner: Preparation is the best kept secret of worry.

Snack: Preparation is a talent.

Misplaced Focus		Negative Result	Redirected Focus		Positive Result
#1: Doubt	»	Paralysis	Presence	»	Passion
#2: Complacency	»	Pain	Engagement	»	Positive Expectation
#3 Blame	»	Powerlessness/ Problems	Resourcefulness	»	Possibilities
#4 Indecision	»	Procrastination	Action	»	Progress
#5: Selfishness	»	Guilt	Service	»	Peace of Mind

DAY 13

Breakfast: Preparation is a temporary act intended to guide.

Lunch: Preparation is a universal language of decision.

Dinner: The keys to the kingdom unlock hell without the right preparation.

Snack: Preparation in youth never ends.

Misplaced Focus		Negative Result	Redirected Focus		Positive Result
#1: Doubt	◆》	Paralysis	Presence	◆》	Passion
#2: Complacency	◆》	Pain	Engagement	◆》	Positive Expectation
#3 Blame	◆》	Powerlessness/ Problems	Resourcefulness	◆》	Possibilities
#4 Indecision	◆》	Procrastination	Action	◆》	Progress
#5: Selfishness	◆》	Guilt	Service	◆》	Peace of Mind

DAY 14

Breakfast: If you want to try acid what part of preparation are you confused about?

Lunch: If preparation causes you to experience anxiety, anticipation might be a struggle for you.

Dinner: Anywhere preparation is taken seriously property values rise.

Snack: If battle is unavoidable, preparation is a useful weapon.

Misplaced Focus		Negative Result	Redirected Focus		Positive Result
#1: Doubt	⟫	Paralysis	Presence	⟫	Passion
#2: Complacency	⟫	Pain	Engagement	⟫	Positive Expectation
#3 Blame	⟫	Powerlessness/ Problems	Resourcefulness	⟫	Possibilities
#4 Indecision	⟫	Procrastination	Action	⟫	Progress
#5: Selfishness	⟫	Guilt	Service	⟫	Peace of Mind

DAY 15

Breakfast: No amount of preparation will help you handle a high maintenance/low self-esteem individual.

Lunch: Beer is a liquid example of preparation.

Dinner: Preparation that negatively impacts belief in self is a blessing in bad vibes.

Snack: Failure is the saving grace of preparation.

Misplaced Focus		Negative Result	Redirected Focus		Positive Result
#1: Doubt	◆》	Paralysis	Presence	◆》	Passion
#2: Complacency	◆》	Pain	Engagement	◆》	Positive Expectation
#3 Blame	◆》	Powerlessness/ Problems	Resourcefulness	◆》	Possibilities
#4 Indecision	◆》	Procrastination	Action	◆》	Progress
#5: Selfishness	◆》	Guilt	Service	◆》	Peace of Mind

DAY 16

Breakfast: Right now is the best time to look at preparation for what it is.

Lunch: Science is the preparation of precision.

Dinner: Simple preparation will do.

Snack: Hopefully one day politics will involve preparation.

Misplaced Focus		Negative Result	Redirected Focus		Positive Result
#1: Doubt	◆》	Paralysis	Presence	◆》	Passion
#2: Complacency	◆》	Pain	Engagement	◆》	Positive Expectation
#3 Blame	◆》	Powerlessness/ Problems	Resourcefulness	◆》	Possibilities
#4 Indecision	◆》	Procrastination	Action	◆》	Progress
#5: Selfishness	◆》	Guilt	Service	◆》	Peace of Mind

DAY 17

Breakfast: If improvement is desired, preparation is a good place to start.

Lunch: If preparation is the last thing to be mentioned followed with "let's hope for the best," enjoy the show.

Dinner: Routine preparation with consistent results chases success.

Snack: Make preparation uncomfortable.

Misplaced Focus		Negative Result	Redirected Focus		Positive Result
#1: Doubt	◆》	Paralysis	Presence	◆》	Passion
#2: Complacency	◆》	Pain	Engagement	◆》	Positive Expectation
#3 Blame	◆》	Powerlessness/ Problems	Resourcefulness	◆》	Possibilities
#4 Indecision	◆》	Procrastination	Action	◆》	Progress
#5: Selfishness	◆》	Guilt	Service	◆》	Peace of Mind

DAY 18

Breakfast: Careful preparation isn't worth the risk.

Lunch: Preparation that identifies weakness deserves a little recognition.

Dinner: In a conflict preparation might create doubt.

Snack: Taking notes is preparation for dependency.

Misplaced Focus		Negative Result	Redirected Focus		Positive Result
#1: Doubt	◆»	Paralysis	Presence	◆»	Passion
#2: Complacency	◆»	Pain	Engagement	◆»	Positive Expectation
#3 Blame	◆»	Powerlessness/ Problems	Resourcefulness	◆»	Possibilities
#4 Indecision	◆»	Procrastination	Action	◆»	Progress
#5: Selfishness	◆»	Guilt	Service	◆»	Peace of Mind

DAY 19

Breakfast: Preparation leaves clues.

Lunch: Life coaches are good with preparation.

Dinner: Even with the best preparation, collapse is possible.

Snack: College is preparation for systematic confusion.

Misplaced Focus		Negative Result	Redirected Focus		Positive Result
#1: Doubt	◆》	Paralysis	Presence	◆》	Passion
#2: Complacency	◆》	Pain	Engagement	◆》	Positive Expectation
#3 Blame	◆》	Powerlessness/ Problems	Resourcefulness	◆》	Possibilities
#4 Indecision	◆》	Procrastination	Action	◆》	Progress
#5: Selfishness	◆》	Guilt	Service	◆》	Peace of Mind

DAY 20

Breakfast: Dysfunction has a good sense of preparation.

Lunch: Preparation is wood in the fire of competitiveness.

Dinner: Expected delays are consequences of preparation.

Snack: A convincing display of preparation is worth discussion.

Misplaced Focus		Negative Result	Redirected Focus		Positive Result
#1: Doubt	◆》	Paralysis	Presence	◆》	Passion
#2: Complacency	◆》	Pain	Engagement	◆》	Positive Expectation
#3 Blame	◆》	Powerlessness/ Problems	Resourcefulness	◆》	Possibilities
#4 Indecision	◆》	Procrastination	Action	◆》	Progress
#5: Selfishness	◆》	Guilt	Service	◆》	Peace of Mind

DAY 21

Breakfast: Hindsight is a skid mark on the underpants of preparation.

Lunch: Educational efficiency is a metric only preparation can appreciate.

Dinner: High effort in preparation shows up as
low expectations regarding defeat.

Snack: Preparation likely won't make you famous.

Misplaced Focus		Negative Result	Redirected Focus		Positive Result
#1: Doubt	◆》	Paralysis	Presence	◆》	Passion
#2: Complacency	◆》	Pain	Engagement	◆》	Positive Expectation
#3 Blame	◆》	Powerlessness/ Problems	Resourcefulness	◆》	Possibilities
#4 Indecision	◆》	Procrastination	Action	◆》	Progress
#5: Selfishness	◆》	Guilt	Service	◆》	Peace of Mind

DAY 22

Breakfast: Make preparation a personal goal for at least one year.

Lunch: Health is not wealth; it is preparation for life.

Dinner: The task of preparation belongs to all but none.

Snack: The villain is better at preparation but usually lacks strength.

Misplaced Focus		Negative Result	Redirected Focus		Positive Result
#1: Doubt	◆》	Paralysis	Presence	◆》	Passion
#2: Complacency	◆》	Pain	Engagement	◆》	Positive Expectation
#3 Blame	◆》	Powerlessness/ Problems	Resourcefulness	◆》	Possibilities
#4 Indecision	◆》	Procrastination	Action	◆》	Progress
#5: Selfishness	◆》	Guilt	Service	◆》	Peace of Mind

DAY 23

Breakfast: Preparation of the soul now comes with a turbo engine.

Lunch: At the heart of preparation is ice.

Dinner: Commitment to preparation is important.

Snack: Instead of rushing through life, adopt preparation and start a family.

Misplaced Focus		Negative Result	Redirected Focus		Positive Result
#1: Doubt	◆》	Paralysis	Presence	◆》	Passion
#2: Complacency	◆》	Pain	Engagement	◆》	Positive Expectation
#3 Blame	◆》	Powerlessness/ Problems	Resourcefulness	◆》	Possibilities
#4 Indecision	◆》	Procrastination	Action	◆》	Progress
#5: Selfishness	◆》	Guilt	Service	◆》	Peace of Mind

DAY 24

Breakfast: Keep going even if the preparation has failed.

Lunch: Preparation for mental storms is a real thing too.

Dinner: Exposure to opportunities without the right preparation looks like competition.

Snack: Exhaustion is good preparation for normal.

Misplaced Focus		Negative Result	Redirected Focus		Positive Result
#1: Doubt	◆》	Paralysis	Presence	◆》	Passion
#2: Complacency	◆》	Pain	Engagement	◆》	Positive Expectation
#3 Blame	◆》	Powerlessness/ Problems	Resourcefulness	◆》	Possibilities
#4 Indecision	◆》	Procrastination	Action	◆》	Progress
#5: Selfishness	◆》	Guilt	Service	◆》	Peace of Mind

DAY 25

Breakfast: Puzzles of preparation are intellectual exercises.

Lunch: Preparation is an excellent negotiation tactic.

Dinner: Accomplishment without preparation feels insignificant.

Snack: Wondering "what if" with or without preparation is a brain fart.

Misplaced Focus		Negative Result	Redirected Focus		Positive Result
#1: Doubt	◆》	Paralysis	Presence	◆》	Passion
#2: Complacency	◆》	Pain	Engagement	◆》	Positive Expectation
#3 Blame	◆》	Powerlessness/ Problems	Resourcefulness	◆》	Possibilities
#4 Indecision	◆》	Procrastination	Action	◆》	Progress
#5: Selfishness	◆》	Guilt	Service	◆》	Peace of Mind

DAY 26

Breakfast: When the desired result is more important than excuses, preparation is worth more than gold.

Lunch: False confidence has experienced preparation as well.

Dinner: Knowing yourself is hard work; why not voluntarily do the preparation before being forced by unknown circumstances?

Snack: Don't let compliments override preparation.

Misplaced Focus		Negative Result	Redirected Focus		Positive Result
#1: Doubt	◆》	Paralysis	Presence	◆》	Passion
#2: Complacency	◆》	Pain	Engagement	◆》	Positive Expectation
#3 Blame	◆》	Powerlessness/ Problems	Resourcefulness	◆》	Possibilities
#4 Indecision	◆》	Procrastination	Action	◆》	Progress
#5: Selfishness	◆》	Guilt	Service	◆》	Peace of Mind

DAY 27

Breakfast: Don't be surprised if your biggest improvement comes from your smallest preparation.

Lunch: Iconic preparation is what makes the world spin.

Dinner: Preparation>Passion.

Snack: Appraisals are values of preparation.

Misplaced Focus		Negative Result	Redirected Focus		Positive Result
#1: Doubt	◆》	Paralysis	Presence	◆》	Passion
#2: Complacency	◆》	Pain	Engagement	◆》	Positive Expectation
#3 Blame	◆》	Powerlessness/ Problems	Resourcefulness	◆》	Possibilities
#4 Indecision	◆》	Procrastination	Action	◆》	Progress
#5: Selfishness	◆》	Guilt	Service	◆》	Peace of Mind

DAY 28

Breakfast: Falling off the map focuses on preparation and coming back with the stories.

Lunch: The most relevant messaging in history misses the mark without preparation.

Dinner: A deck of cards and preparation can change the world.

Snack: Preparing to train is training preparation.

Misplaced Focus		Negative Result	Redirected Focus		Positive Result
#1: Doubt	⟫	Paralysis	Presence	⟫	Passion
#2: Complacency	⟫	Pain	Engagement	⟫	Positive Expectation
#3 Blame	⟫	Powerlessness/ Problems	Resourcefulness	⟫	Possibilities
#4 Indecision	⟫	Procrastination	Action	⟫	Progress
#5: Selfishness	⟫	Guilt	Service	⟫	Peace of Mind

DAY 29

Breakfast: Preparation does not carry luggage.

Lunch: All the failed attempts make preparation successful.

Dinner: 24/7 365 are the numbers related to opportunities for preparation.

Snack: The internet is simply a preparation tool.

Misplaced Focus		Negative Result	Redirected Focus		Positive Result
#1: Doubt	◆»	Paralysis	Presence	◆»	Passion
#2: Complacency	◆»	Pain	Engagement	◆»	Positive Expectation
#3 Blame	◆»	Powerlessness/ Problems	Resourcefulness	◆»	Possibilities
#4 Indecision	◆»	Procrastination	Action	◆»	Progress
#5: Selfishness	◆»	Guilt	Service	◆»	Peace of Mind

DAY 30

Breakfast: Invasion of privacy is preparation for a throne.

Lunch: Learning preparation skills gain attention.

Dinner: Noise filtered through preparation is beauty.

Snack: Dreams are preparation for reality if you're brave enough.

Misplaced Focus		Negative Result	Redirected Focus		Positive Result
#1: Doubt	◆》	Paralysis	Presence	◆》	Passion
#2: Complacency	◆》	Pain	Engagement	◆》	Positive Expectation
#3 Blame	◆》	Powerlessness/ Problems	Resourcefulness	◆》	Possibilities
#4 Indecision	◆》	Procrastination	Action	◆》	Progress
#5: Selfishness	◆》	Guilt	Service	◆》	Peace of Mind

DAY 31

Breakfast: Some might not ever see value in libraries or preparation.

Lunch: Preparation is a form of forgiveness for past ignorance.

Dinner: Domination divided by preparation is simple mathematics.

Snack: Complaining too soon only makes preparation look better.

Misplaced Focus		Negative Result	Redirected Focus		Positive Result
#1: Doubt	◆»	Paralysis	Presence	◆»	Passion
#2: Complacency	◆»	Pain	Engagement	◆»	Positive Expectation
#3 Blame	◆»	Powerlessness/ Problems	Resourcefulness	◆»	Possibilities
#4 Indecision	◆»	Procrastination	Action	◆»	Progress
#5: Selfishness	◆»	Guilt	Service	◆»	Peace of Mind

DAY 32

Breakfast: If preparation gives you peace of mind, work harder.

Lunch: With enough time and preparation you will get sued.

Dinner: Dumb luck is more fun than preparation.

Snack: Preparation is currently measured in news headlines.

Misplaced Focus	Negative Result	Redirected Focus	Positive Result
#1: Doubt	Paralysis	Presence	Passion
#2: Complacency	Pain	Engagement	Positive Expectation
#3 Blame	Powerlessness/ Problems	Resourcefulness	Possibilities
#4 Indecision	Procrastination	Action	Progress
#5: Selfishness	Guilt	Service	Peace of Mind

DAY 33

Breakfast: Why does preparation for litigation feel like constipation?

Lunch: Put everything into preparation and see if your name comes up.

Dinner: Not going to lie; preparation quotes are tough to think of on the spot.

Snack: Direction is more important than speed even with perfect preparation.

Misplaced Focus		Negative Result	Redirected Focus		Positive Result
#1: Doubt	◆》	Paralysis	Presence	◆》	Passion
#2: Complacency	◆》	Pain	Engagement	◆》	Positive Expectation
#3 Blame	◆》	Powerlessness/ Problems	Resourcefulness	◆》	Possibilities
#4 Indecision	◆》	Procrastination	Action	◆》	Progress
#5: Selfishness	◆》	Guilt	Service	◆》	Peace of Mind

DAY 34

Breakfast: Don't lower expectations before increasing preparation.

Lunch: Aim to follow preparation more than popularity.

Dinner: Possibilities are held hostage by lazy preparation.

Snack: A common manipulation regarding preparation is success.

Misplaced Focus		Negative Result	Redirected Focus		Positive Result
#1: Doubt	◆》	Paralysis	Presence	◆》	Passion
#2: Complacency	◆》	Pain	Engagement	◆》	Positive Expectation
#3 Blame	◆》	Powerlessness/ Problems	Resourcefulness	◆》	Possibilities
#4 Indecision	◆》	Procrastination	Action	◆》	Progress
#5: Selfishness	◆》	Guilt	Service	◆》	Peace of Mind

DAY 35

Breakfast: Careless preparation has an expiration date.

Lunch: On average a person uses around 20,000 words in their lifetime; preparation is dangerously rare.

Dinner: The choir sings whatever preparation brings.

Snack: Samples are proof that preparation sells.

Misplaced Focus	Negative Result	Redirected Focus	Positive Result
#1: Doubt	Paralysis	Presence	Passion
#2: Complacency	Pain	Engagement	Positive Expectation
#3 Blame	Powerlessness/ Problems	Resourcefulness	Possibilities
#4 Indecision	Procrastination	Action	Progress
#5: Selfishness	Guilt	Service	Peace of Mind

DAY 36

Breakfast: Identifying threats is just good preparation.

Lunch: Forward momentum is mostly preparation and belief.

Dinner: Preparation is a member of a secret society.

Snack: Fear treats preparation like a side dish.

Misplaced Focus		Negative Result	Redirected Focus		Positive Result
#1: Doubt	»	Paralysis	Presence	»	Passion
#2: Complacency	»	Pain	Engagement	»	Positive Expectation
#3 Blame	»	Powerlessness/ Problems	Resourcefulness	»	Possibilities
#4 Indecision	»	Procrastination	Action	»	Progress
#5: Selfishness	»	Guilt	Service	»	Peace of Mind

DAY 37

Breakfast: Some cycles can't be broken by preparation alone.

Lunch: Interference during preparation is good practice.

Dinner: Preparation allows you to be the most interesting while saying the least.

Snack: Moderation during preparation creates complications.

Misplaced Focus		Negative Result	Redirected Focus		Positive Result
#1: Doubt	◆》	Paralysis	Presence	◆》	Passion
#2: Complacency	◆》	Pain	Engagement	◆》	Positive Expectation
#3 Blame	◆》	Powerlessness/ Problems	Resourcefulness	◆》	Possibilities
#4 Indecision	◆》	Procrastination	Action	◆》	Progress
#5: Selfishness	◆》	Guilt	Service	◆》	Peace of Mind

DAY 38

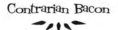

Breakfast: In the game of Chess, preparation is an illusion.

Lunch: Preparation is the best way to start a relationship.

Dinner: The naked truth is immune to preparation.

Snack: Staying ready is the catalyst to preparation.

Misplaced Focus	Negative Result	Redirected Focus	Positive Result
#1: Doubt	Paralysis	Presence	Passion
#2: Complacency	Pain	Engagement	Positive Expectation
#3 Blame	Powerlessness/ Problems	Resourcefulness	Possibilities
#4 Indecision	Procrastination	Action	Progress
#5: Selfishness	Guilt	Service	Peace of Mind

DAY 39

Breakfast: All the good ideas that involve preparation are already taken.

Lunch: Do the preparation or be the preparation.

Dinner: Creations from preparation are guilt free.

Snack: The stories we tell ourselves rarely involve preparation.

Misplaced Focus		Negative Result	Redirected Focus		Positive Result
#1: Doubt	◆》	Paralysis	Presence	◆》	Passion
#2: Complacency	◆》	Pain	Engagement	◆》	Positive Expectation
#3 Blame	◆》	Powerlessness/ Problems	Resourcefulness	◆》	Possibilities
#4 Indecision	◆》	Procrastination	Action	◆》	Progress
#5: Selfishness	◆》	Guilt	Service	◆》	Peace of Mind

DAY 40

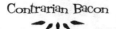

Breakfast: Nobody owes you anything, but preparation has a few rain checks.

Lunch: Peace enhances preparation.

Dinner: Preparation that rapidly declines under pressure still has purpose.

Snack: The lies surrounding preparation have concealed identities.

Misplaced Focus		Negative Result	Redirected Focus		Positive Result
#1: Doubt	◆》	Paralysis	Presence	◆》	Passion
#2: Complacency	◆》	Pain	Engagement	◆》	Positive Expectation
#3 Blame	◆》	Powerlessness/ Problems	Resourcefulness	◆》	Possibilities
#4 Indecision	◆》	Procrastination	Action	◆》	Progress
#5: Selfishness	◆》	Guilt	Service	◆》	Peace of Mind

DAY 41

Breakfast: The rhythm of preparation is followed by a select few.

Lunch: A second of preparation is better than a day of wasted energy.

Dinner: The time used for preparation is neither lost nor gained.

Snack: Until preparation is highly valued, up is down and down is up.

Misplaced Focus		Negative Result	Redirected Focus		Positive Result
#1: Doubt	◆»	Paralysis	Presence	◆»	Passion
#2: Complacency	◆»	Pain	Engagement	◆»	Positive Expectation
#3 Blame	◆»	Powerlessness/ Problems	Resourcefulness	◆»	Possibilities
#4 Indecision	◆»	Procrastination	Action	◆»	Progress
#5: Selfishness	◆»	Guilt	Service	◆»	Peace of Mind

DAY 42

Breakfast: If there is an urge for preparation, claim what you seek.

Lunch: Violence is the weakest form of preparation.

Dinner: If you wait too long preparation becomes a chore.

Snack: The right questions send a warm welcome to preparation.

Misplaced Focus		Negative Result	Redirected Focus		Positive Result
#1: Doubt	◆»	Paralysis	Presence	◆»	Passion
#2: Complacency	◆»	Pain	Engagement	◆»	Positive Expectation
#3 Blame	◆»	Powerlessness/ Problems	Resourcefulness	◆»	Possibilities
#4 Indecision	◆»	Procrastination	Action	◆»	Progress
#5: Selfishness	◆»	Guilt	Service	◆»	Peace of Mind

DAY 43

Breakfast: Preparation is access to advanced operation.

Lunch: Preparation molds you into the architect of results.

Dinner: Preparation is self love.

Snack: Find a way to make preparation fun and play to train.

Misplaced Focus		Negative Result	Redirected Focus		Positive Result
#1: Doubt	◆》	Paralysis	Presence	◆》	Passion
#2: Complacency	◆》	Pain	Engagement	◆》	Positive Expectation
#3 Blame	◆》	Powerlessness/ Problems	Resourcefulness	◆》	Possibilities
#4 Indecision	◆》	Procrastination	Action	◆》	Progress
#5: Selfishness	◆》	Guilt	Service	◆》	Peace of Mind

DAY 44

Breakfast: If all eyes are on your preparation, victory is certain.

Lunch: Let preparation be part of your identity.

Dinner: No need to say much if preparation is the focus.

Snack: Preparation of food is a common interest.

Misplaced Focus		Negative Result	Redirected Focus		Positive Result
#1: Doubt	◆»	Paralysis	Presence	◆»	Passion
#2: Complacency	◆»	Pain	Engagement	◆»	Positive Expectation
#3 Blame	◆»	Powerlessness/ Problems	Resourcefulness	◆»	Possibilities
#4 Indecision	◆»	Procrastination	Action	◆»	Progress
#5: Selfishness	◆»	Guilt	Service	◆»	Peace of Mind

DAY 45

Breakfast: Being left behind extends the reach of preparation.

Lunch: Attention to detail regarding preparation is everything.

Dinner: You were not born to complain—let preparation be your voice.

Snack: Bottled-up emotions can and should be used during preparation.

Misplaced Focus		Negative Result	Redirected Focus		Positive Result
#1: Doubt	◆»	Paralysis	Presence	◆»	Passion
#2: Complacency	◆»	Pain	Engagement	◆»	Positive Expectation
#3 Blame	◆»	Powerlessness/ Problems	Resourcefulness	◆»	Possibilities
#4 Indecision	◆»	Procrastination	Action	◆»	Progress
#5: Selfishness	◆»	Guilt	Service	◆»	Peace of Mind

DAY 46

Breakfast: To fully appreciate a moment, usually some type of preparation has taken place.

Lunch: Preparation is an awful solution.

Dinner: An automotive vehicle is the finest example of preparation there is.

Snack: Cheap preparation, cheap performance.

Misplaced Focus		Negative Result	Redirected Focus		Positive Result
#1: Doubt	◆》	Paralysis	Presence	◆》	Passion
#2: Complacency	◆》	Pain	Engagement	◆》	Positive Expectation
#3 Blame	◆》	Powerlessness/ Problems	Resourcefulness	◆》	Possibilities
#4 Indecision	◆》	Procrastination	Action	◆》	Progress
#5: Selfishness	◆》	Guilt	Service	◆》	Peace of Mind

DAY 47

Breakfast: Avoid letting preparation overwhelm you into stagnation.

Lunch: Constantly consuming anything with preparation ignites the imagination.

Dinner: The more you prepare, the more preparation influences.

Snack: Credit given for preparation translates into mistakes during action.

Misplaced Focus		Negative Result	Redirected Focus		Positive Result
#1: Doubt	◆》	Paralysis	Presence	◆》	Passion
#2: Complacency	◆》	Pain	Engagement	◆》	Positive Expectation
#3 Blame	◆》	Powerlessness/ Problems	Resourcefulness	◆》	Possibilities
#4 Indecision	◆》	Procrastination	Action	◆》	Progress
#5: Selfishness	◆》	Guilt	Service	◆》	Peace of Mind

DAY 48

Breakfast: Nobody cares about individual preparation.

Lunch: I am convinced that preparation is a good thing.

Dinner: Sometimes step by step is all the preparation needed.

Snack: Preparation is the reason it isn't over until it's over.

Misplaced Focus		Negative Result	Redirected Focus		Positive Result
#1: Doubt	◆》	Paralysis	Presence	◆》	Passion
#2: Complacency	◆》	Pain	Engagement	◆》	Positive Expectation
#3 Blame	◆》	Powerlessness/ Problems	Resourcefulness	◆》	Possibilities
#4 Indecision	◆》	Procrastination	Action	◆》	Progress
#5: Selfishness	◆》	Guilt	Service	◆》	Peace of Mind

DAY 49

Breakfast: Find a craft that makes preparation fun.

Lunch: Not much outside of preparation other than obscurity and inclusion.

Dinner: Going with the flow makes preparation look like comedy.

Snack: Anything of significance leverages preparation.

Misplaced Focus		Negative Result	Redirected Focus		Positive Result
#1: Doubt	◆》	Paralysis	Presence	◆》	Passion
#2: Complacency	◆》	Pain	Engagement	◆》	Positive Expectation
#3 Blame	◆》	Powerlessness/ Problems	Resourcefulness	◆》	Possibilities
#4 Indecision	◆》	Procrastination	Action	◆》	Progress
#5: Selfishness	◆》	Guilt	Service	◆》	Peace of Mind

DAY 50

Breakfast: Crisis is the Queen of preparation.

Lunch: Getting deeply lost in preparation secures belief.

Dinner: A diet without preparation is a pizza away from disaster.

Snack: Keep going; preparation and hard work pay well.

Misplaced Focus		Negative Result	Redirected Focus		Positive Result
#1: Doubt	◆》	Paralysis	Presence	◆》	Passion
#2: Complacency	◆》	Pain	Engagement	◆》	Positive Expectation
#3 Blame	◆》	Powerlessness/ Problems	Resourcefulness	◆》	Possibilities
#4 Indecision	◆》	Procrastination	Action	◆》	Progress
#5: Selfishness	◆》	Guilt	Service	◆》	Peace of Mind

DAY 51

Breakfast: Entertainment embraces preparation well.

Lunch: Recovery is a gray area of preparation.

Dinner: Historical data suggests preparation is a good idea.

Snack: Impressive is that which is done with very little obvious preparation.

Misplaced Focus		Negative Result	Redirected Focus		Positive Result
#1: Doubt	⟫	Paralysis	Presence	⟫	Passion
#2: Complacency	⟫	Pain	Engagement	⟫	Positive Expectation
#3 Blame	⟫	Powerlessness/ Problems	Resourcefulness	⟫	Possibilities
#4 Indecision	⟫	Procrastination	Action	⟫	Progress
#5: Selfishness	⟫	Guilt	Service	⟫	Peace of Mind

DAY 52

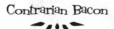

Breakfast: Preparation while everyone sleeps is the standard.

Lunch: The importance of preparation needs to be televised.

Dinner: Amazing what rest and relaxation can do for the preparation process.

Snack: Keeping a journal is interactive preparation.

Misplaced Focus	Negative Result	Redirected Focus	Positive Result
#1: Doubt	Paralysis	Presence	Passion
#2: Complacency	Pain	Engagement	Positive Expectation
#3 Blame	Powerlessness/ Problems	Resourcefulness	Possibilities
#4 Indecision	Procrastination	Action	Progress
#5: Selfishness	Guilt	Service	Peace of Mind

DAY 53

Breakfast: A knife is a preparation device that uses people.

Lunch: If two people are battling for your attention, use faith as preparation.

Dinner: The labor of preparation in most situations is a labor of love.

Snack: In a laboratory, preparation is the only experiment.

Misplaced Focus		Negative Result	Redirected Focus		Positive Result
#1: Doubt	◆》	Paralysis	Presence	◆》	Passion
#2: Complacency	◆》	Pain	Engagement	◆》	Positive Expectation
#3 Blame	◆》	Powerlessness/ Problems	Resourcefulness	◆》	Possibilities
#4 Indecision	◆》	Procrastination	Action	◆》	Progress
#5: Selfishness	◆》	Guilt	Service	◆》	Peace of Mind

DAY 54

Breakfast: When preparation is largely voluntary, the associated work has a life of its own.

Lunch: To successfully maintain multiple relationships, preparation is not the answer.

Dinner: Negotiation of preparation is a painful situation.

Snack: Preparation occurs immediately.

Misplaced Focus		Negative Result	Redirected Focus		Positive Result
#1: Doubt	◆》	Paralysis	Presence	◆》	Passion
#2: Complacency	◆》	Pain	Engagement	◆》	Positive Expectation
#3 Blame	◆》	Powerlessness/ Problems	Resourcefulness	◆》	Possibilities
#4 Indecision	◆》	Procrastination	Action	◆》	Progress
#5: Selfishness	◆》	Guilt	Service	◆》	Peace of Mind

DAY 55

Breakfast: Offers that leverage preparation are more appealing.

Lunch: Preparation organizes operation and simplifies dedication.

Dinner: Preparation was originally known as "In the beginning."

Snack: Preparation without nonchalant beliefs would be catastrophic.

Misplaced Focus		Negative Result	Redirected Focus		Positive Result
#1: Doubt	◆》	Paralysis	Presence	◆》	Passion
#2: Complacency	◆》	Pain	Engagement	◆》	Positive Expectation
#3 Blame	◆》	Powerlessness/ Problems	Resourcefulness	◆》	Possibilities
#4 Indecision	◆》	Procrastination	Action	◆》	Progress
#5: Selfishness	◆》	Guilt	Service	◆》	Peace of Mind

DAY 56

Breakfast: Obsession with preparation becomes religion.

Lunch: Habits are pawns of preparation.

Dinner: Wanting it and working for it both come from preparation of character.

Snack: Just because you like it does not mean it is good preparation.

Misplaced Focus		Negative Result	Redirected Focus		Positive Result
#1: Doubt	◆》	Paralysis	Presence	◆》	Passion
#2: Complacency	◆》	Pain	Engagement	◆》	Positive Expectation
#3 Blame	◆》	Powerlessness/ Problems	Resourcefulness	◆》	Possibilities
#4 Indecision	◆》	Procrastination	Action	◆》	Progress
#5: Selfishness	◆》	Guilt	Service	◆》	Peace of Mind

DAY 57

Breakfast: Those who prepare the most are slaves to preparation.

Lunch: Until personal experience guides you, use preparation as a temporary foundation.

Dinner: Preparation is important but at some point, your only concern should be performance.

Snack: Mass projection of internal conflict is preparation gone wrong.

Misplaced Focus		Negative Result	Redirected Focus		Positive Result
#1: Doubt	◆»	Paralysis	Presence	◆»	Passion
#2: Complacency	◆»	Pain	Engagement	◆»	Positive Expectation
#3 Blame	◆»	Powerlessness/ Problems	Resourcefulness	◆»	Possibilities
#4 Indecision	◆»	Procrastination	Action	◆»	Progress
#5: Selfishness	◆»	Guilt	Service	◆»	Peace of Mind

DAY 58

Breakfast: Prayers preserve life and preparation confirms.

Lunch: Strategic preparation is a joke.

Dinner: With proper preparation, results should be tied to you alone.

Snack: Positions of power without preparation disrespect silence.

Misplaced Focus		Negative Result	Redirected Focus		Positive Result
#1: Doubt	◆》	Paralysis	Presence	◆》	Passion
#2: Complacency	◆》	Pain	Engagement	◆》	Positive Expectation
#3 Blame	◆》	Powerlessness/ Problems	Resourcefulness	◆》	Possibilities
#4 Indecision	◆》	Procrastination	Action	◆》	Progress
#5: Selfishness	◆》	Guilt	Service	◆》	Peace of Mind

DAY 59

Breakfast: Asking how something happened is good reporting and even better preparation.

Lunch: Everyday won't be sunshine and butterflies, but the caterpillar loves preparation.

Dinner: I agree with 90% of my social media posts from 10 years ago; preparation is bullshit.

Snack: Preparation is the kiss that gets the girl.

Misplaced Focus		Negative Result	Redirected Focus		Positive Result
#1: Doubt	◆》	Paralysis	Presence	◆》	Passion
#2: Complacency	◆》	Pain	Engagement	◆》	Positive Expectation
#3 Blame	◆》	Powerlessness/ Problems	Resourcefulness	◆》	Possibilities
#4 Indecision	◆》	Procrastination	Action	◆》	Progress
#5: Selfishness	◆》	Guilt	Service	◆》	Peace of Mind

DAY 60

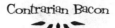

Breakfast: Thorough preparation should create the illusion that you are The President of the United States of America.

Lunch: Preparation without commitment is aimless energy.

Dinner: Effective preparation produces clarity and brevity.

Snack: If friendly preparation is worst case scenario, marijuana is a national hero.

Misplaced Focus		Negative Result	Redirected Focus		Positive Result
#1: Doubt	»	Paralysis	Presence	»	Passion
#2: Complacency	»	Pain	Engagement	»	Positive Expectation
#3 Blame	»	Powerlessness/ Problems	Resourcefulness	»	Possibilities
#4 Indecision	»	Procrastination	Action	»	Progress
#5: Selfishness	»	Guilt	Service	»	Peace of Mind

DAY 61

Breakfast: Possibilities are endless until preparation becomes the focus.

Lunch: The cleanest preparation is a closed loop process.

Dinner: Encourage preparation often in troubling times.

Snack: Getting pinched is the best part of preparation.

Misplaced Focus		Negative Result	Redirected Focus		Positive Result
#1: Doubt	◆》	Paralysis	Presence	◆》	Passion
#2: Complacency	◆》	Pain	Engagement	◆》	Positive Expectation
#3 Blame	◆》	Powerlessness/ Problems	Resourcefulness	◆》	Possibilities
#4 Indecision	◆》	Procrastination	Action	◆》	Progress
#5: Selfishness	◆》	Guilt	Service	◆》	Peace of Mind

DAY 62

Breakfast: Preparation in the jungle applies to civilization.

Lunch: Regular preparation is mental masturbation.

Dinner: Please don't be naïve—massacres are orderly preparation.

Snack: Preparation of lethal force has a captain, not a leader.

Misplaced Focus		Negative Result	Redirected Focus		Positive Result
#1: Doubt	»	Paralysis	Presence	»	Passion
#2: Complacency	»	Pain	Engagement	»	Positive Expectation
#3 Blame	»	Powerlessness/ Problems	Resourcefulness	»	Possibilities
#4 Indecision	»	Procrastination	Action	»	Progress
#5: Selfishness	»	Guilt	Service	»	Peace of Mind

DAY 63

Breakfast: Preparation can be grimy.

Lunch: Streaming services are preparation on steroids.

Dinner: Preparation underground never sees the light.

Snack: Isolation is preparation heaven.

Misplaced Focus		Negative Result	Redirected Focus		Positive Result
#1: Doubt	◆»	Paralysis	Presence	◆»	Passion
#2: Complacency	◆»	Pain	Engagement	◆»	Positive Expectation
#3 Blame	◆»	Powerlessness/ Problems	Resourcefulness	◆»	Possibilities
#4 Indecision	◆»	Procrastination	Action	◆»	Progress
#5: Selfishness	◆»	Guilt	Service	◆»	Peace of Mind

DAY 64

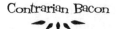

Breakfast: Consistency is the sexiest example of preparation.

Lunch: Personality without preparation is gay.

Dinner: Do or die is the final form of preparation.

Snack: No progress beats slow progress with preparation and life hacks.

Misplaced Focus		Negative Result	Redirected Focus		Positive Result
#1: Doubt	◆》	Paralysis	Presence	◆》	Passion
#2: Complacency	◆》	Pain	Engagement	◆》	Positive Expectation
#3 Blame	◆》	Powerlessness/ Problems	Resourcefulness	◆》	Possibilities
#4 Indecision	◆》	Procrastination	Action	◆》	Progress
#5: Selfishness	◆》	Guilt	Service	◆》	Peace of Mind

DAY 65

Breakfast: Depending on what day it is, muscle needs more work than preparation.

Lunch: Preparation<Presence.

Dinner: Life is worth more than preparation.

Snack: Revival is reverse preparation.

Misplaced Focus		Negative Result	Redirected Focus		Positive Result
#1: Doubt	◆》	Paralysis	Presence	◆》	Passion
#2: Complacency	◆》	Pain	Engagement	◆》	Positive Expectation
#3 Blame	◆》	Powerlessness/ Problems	Resourcefulness	◆》	Possibilities
#4 Indecision	◆》	Procrastination	Action	◆》	Progress
#5: Selfishness	◆》	Guilt	Service	◆》	Peace of Mind

DAY 66

Breakfast: Education translates well into preparation.

Lunch: Let's just say it didn't happen if preparation wasn't our focus.

Dinner: Meditation is the purest preparation I can think of.

Snack: Losing hope is more painful than bad preparation.

Misplaced Focus		Negative Result	Redirected Focus		Positive Result
#1: Doubt	◆⟫	Paralysis	Presence	◆⟫	Passion
#2: Complacency	◆⟫	Pain	Engagement	◆⟫	Positive Expectation
#3 Blame	◆⟫	Powerlessness/ Problems	Resourcefulness	◆⟫	Possibilities
#4 Indecision	◆⟫	Procrastination	Action	◆⟫	Progress
#5: Selfishness	◆⟫	Guilt	Service	◆⟫	Peace of Mind

DAY 67

Breakfast: Yesterday is gone, tomorrow is busy with preparation, and currently squirrels like nuts.

Lunch: When preparation matters anything becomes possible.

Dinner: When you believe you're right about something, take time to observe and validate preparation.

Snack: A need to constantly search exaggerates preparation.

Misplaced Focus		Negative Result	Redirected Focus		Positive Result
#1: Doubt	◆》	Paralysis	Presence	◆》	Passion
#2: Complacency	◆》	Pain	Engagement	◆》	Positive Expectation
#3 Blame	◆》	Powerlessness/ Problems	Resourcefulness	◆》	Possibilities
#4 Indecision	◆》	Procrastination	Action	◆》	Progress
#5: Selfishness	◆》	Guilt	Service	◆》	Peace of Mind

DAY 68

Breakfast: Going faster without the anticipation of preparation is fun, dumb, and wild but more fun.

Lunch: Stop and smell the roses, then get back to preparation for life.

Dinner: Plan categories and avoid preparation.

Snack: Being united is some wild dream or excellent preparation.

Misplaced Focus		Negative Result	Redirected Focus		Positive Result
#1: Doubt	◈	Paralysis	Presence	◈	Passion
#2: Complacency	◈	Pain	Engagement	◈	Positive Expectation
#3 Blame	◈	Powerlessness/ Problems	Resourcefulness	◈	Possibilities
#4 Indecision	◈	Procrastination	Action	◈	Progress
#5: Selfishness	◈	Guilt	Service	◈	Peace of Mind

DAY 69

Breakfast: Greatness doesn't exist without preparation—let's argue!

Lunch: Research and preparation are on fire right now.

Dinner: Nothing too special about preparation, but it works.

Snack: Documentation of preparation changes laws.

Misplaced Focus		Negative Result	Redirected Focus		Positive Result
#1: Doubt	◆⟫	Paralysis	Presence	◆⟫	Passion
#2: Complacency	◆⟫	Pain	Engagement	◆⟫	Positive Expectation
#3 Blame	◆⟫	Powerlessness/ Problems	Resourcefulness	◆⟫	Possibilities
#4 Indecision	◆⟫	Procrastination	Action	◆⟫	Progress
#5: Selfishness	◆⟫	Guilt	Service	◆⟫	Peace of Mind

DAY 70

Breakfast: Do it so well that preparation becomes the only answer.

Lunch: Chaos is good preparation for anything.

Dinner: Virtual and actual preparation eliminate the need for investigation.

Snack: Bulletproof anything is serious preparation.

Misplaced Focus		Negative Result	Redirected Focus		Positive Result
#1: Doubt	◆》	Paralysis	Presence	◆》	Passion
#2: Complacency	◆》	Pain	Engagement	◆》	Positive Expectation
#3 Blame	◆》	Powerlessness/ Problems	Resourcefulness	◆》	Possibilities
#4 Indecision	◆》	Procrastination	Action	◆》	Progress
#5: Selfishness	◆》	Guilt	Service	◆》	Peace of Mind

DAY 71

Breakfast: Influential preparation empowers participants to engage.

Lunch: Happiness found in preparation is worth sharing.

Dinner: If preparation only makes you 1% better, it is a success.

Snack: Developing emotional intelligence makes preparation meaningful.

Misplaced Focus		Negative Result	Redirected Focus		Positive Result
#1: Doubt	◆》	Paralysis	Presence	◆》	Passion
#2: Complacency	◆》	Pain	Engagement	◆》	Positive Expectation
#3 Blame	◆》	Powerlessness/ Problems	Resourcefulness	◆》	Possibilities
#4 Indecision	◆》	Procrastination	Action	◆》	Progress
#5: Selfishness	◆》	Guilt	Service	◆》	Peace of Mind

DAY 72

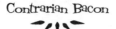

Breakfast: Self love is the ultimate preparation.

Lunch: Affirmation is spiritual preparation.

Dinner: Time management for preparation looks like insecure authority.

Snack: Occasionally the best preparation is taking the road less traveled.

Misplaced Focus		Negative Result	Redirected Focus		Positive Result
#1: Doubt	◆»	Paralysis	Presence	◆»	Passion
#2: Complacency	◆»	Pain	Engagement	◆»	Positive Expectation
#3 Blame	◆»	Powerlessness/ Problems	Resourcefulness	◆»	Possibilities
#4 Indecision	◆»	Procrastination	Action	◆»	Progress
#5: Selfishness	◆»	Guilt	Service	◆»	Peace of Mind

DAY 73

Breakfast: A system built with honest preparation is a good investment.

Lunch: Preparation is the foundation of a bounce back.

Dinner: Preparation is not equal to self discipline.

Snack: Before long, minimal preparation will be all that is needed.

Misplaced Focus		Negative Result	Redirected Focus		Positive Result
#1: Doubt	◆》	Paralysis	Presence	◆》	Passion
#2: Complacency	◆》	Pain	Engagement	◆》	Positive Expectation
#3 Blame	◆》	Powerlessness/ Problems	Resourcefulness	◆》	Possibilities
#4 Indecision	◆》	Procrastination	Action	◆》	Progress
#5: Selfishness	◆》	Guilt	Service	◆》	Peace of Mind

DAY 74

Breakfast: Losing to win is clear preparation.

Lunch: Participation is an indirect brand of preparation.

Dinner: Showmanship is a clue left by preparation.

Snack: Don't be fooled by the numbers: preparation is the 1 thing to be trusted.

Misplaced Focus		Negative Result	Redirected Focus		Positive Result
#1: Doubt	◆》	Paralysis	Presence	◆》	Passion
#2: Complacency	◆》	Pain	Engagement	◆》	Positive Expectation
#3 Blame	◆》	Powerlessness/ Problems	Resourcefulness	◆》	Possibilities
#4 Indecision	◆》	Procrastination	Action	◆》	Progress
#5: Selfishness	◆》	Guilt	Service	◆》	Peace of Mind

DAY 75

Breakfast: Never say "later" in fear of preparation.

Lunch: Bosses use preparation and blueprints.

Dinner: The momentum of life is unstoppable with or without preparation.

Snack: Entrepreneurship has already internalized preparation.

Misplaced Focus		Negative Result	Redirected Focus		Positive Result
#1: Doubt	◆》	Paralysis	Presence	◆》	Passion
#2: Complacency	◆》	Pain	Engagement	◆》	Positive Expectation
#3 Blame	◆》	Powerlessness/ Problems	Resourcefulness	◆》	Possibilities
#4 Indecision	◆》	Procrastination	Action	◆》	Progress
#5: Selfishness	◆》	Guilt	Service	◆》	Peace of Mind

DAY 76

Breakfast: If earning income from your talent sounds too good to be true, there is more preparation waiting to prove you wrong.

Lunch: Preparation is the ghostwriter for the phrase "attitude determines altitude".

Dinner: Relationship marketing is persuasive preparation.

Snack: If they have ever changed your diaper, preparation won't work—go ask somebody else.

Misplaced Focus		Negative Result	Redirected Focus		Positive Result
#1: Doubt	◆》	Paralysis	Presence	◆》	Passion
#2: Complacency	◆》	Pain	Engagement	◆》	Positive Expectation
#3 Blame	◆》	Powerlessness/ Problems	Resourcefulness	◆》	Possibilities
#4 Indecision	◆》	Procrastination	Action	◆》	Progress
#5: Selfishness	◆》	Guilt	Service	◆》	Peace of Mind

DAY 77

Breakfast: Speculation of current information is healthy with preparation.

Lunch: The best prank ever is old fashioned preparation.

Dinner: Profit first is poor preparation.

Snack: I take preparation seriously; I will always use cash to pay taxes.

Misplaced Focus		Negative Result	Redirected Focus		Positive Result
#1: Doubt	◆》	Paralysis	Presence	◆》	Passion
#2: Complacency	◆》	Pain	Engagement	◆》	Positive Expectation
#3 Blame	◆》	Powerlessness/ Problems	Resourcefulness	◆》	Possibilities
#4 Indecision	◆》	Procrastination	Action	◆》	Progress
#5: Selfishness	◆》	Guilt	Service	◆》	Peace of Mind

DAY 78

Breakfast: Location partly determines preparation.

Lunch: Strong communication and preparation contribute to growth.

Dinner: If the planned path is blocked and panic occurs, don't blame preparation.

Snack: Reaction time is a reflection of preparation.

Misplaced Focus		Negative Result	Redirected Focus		Positive Result
#1: Doubt	◆》	Paralysis	Presence	◆》	Passion
#2: Complacency	◆》	Pain	Engagement	◆》	Positive Expectation
#3 Blame	◆》	Powerlessness/ Problems	Resourcefulness	◆》	Possibilities
#4 Indecision	◆》	Procrastination	Action	◆》	Progress
#5: Selfishness	◆》	Guilt	Service	◆》	Peace of Mind

DAY 79

Breakfast: Unwanted thoughts can't win against real preparation.

Lunch: The preparation to excuse ratio is undefined.

Dinner: Safety first is the mother of preparation.

Snack: Terror is the aftermath of guaranteed preparation.

Misplaced Focus		Negative Result	Redirected Focus		Positive Result
#1: Doubt	◆》	Paralysis	Presence	◆》	Passion
#2: Complacency	◆》	Pain	Engagement	◆》	Positive Expectation
#3 Blame	◆》	Powerlessness/ Problems	Resourcefulness	◆》	Possibilities
#4 Indecision	◆》	Procrastination	Action	◆》	Progress
#5: Selfishness	◆》	Guilt	Service	◆》	Peace of Mind

DAY 80

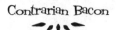

Breakfast: You can have it all with no preparation—it's known as hallucination.

Lunch: When a situation is unable to be changed, preparation is mandatory.

Dinner: Going your own way should be traditional preparation.

Snack: Preparation indicates that suffering is the elixir of life.

Misplaced Focus		Negative Result	Redirected Focus		Positive Result
#1: Doubt	»	Paralysis	Presence	»	Passion
#2: Complacency	»	Pain	Engagement	»	Positive Expectation
#3 Blame	»	Powerlessness/ Problems	Resourcefulness	»	Possibilities
#4 Indecision	»	Procrastination	Action	»	Progress
#5: Selfishness	»	Guilt	Service	»	Peace of Mind

DAY 81

Breakfast: To understand destruction is to understand preparation.

Lunch: Endurance from preparation sustains life.

Dinner: When the desire for preparation outweighs doubt and fear, progress is possible.

Snack: Lack of meaning and purpose follows preparation everywhere.

Misplaced Focus		Negative Result	Redirected Focus		Positive Result
#1: Doubt	◆»	Paralysis	Presence	◆»	Passion
#2: Complacency	◆»	Pain	Engagement	◆»	Positive Expectation
#3 Blame	◆»	Powerlessness/ Problems	Resourcefulness	◆»	Possibilities
#4 Indecision	◆»	Procrastination	Action	◆»	Progress
#5: Selfishness	◆»	Guilt	Service	◆»	Peace of Mind

DAY 82

Breakfast: Losing teaches lessons of preparation, winning teaches lessons of primal habits.

Lunch: Personal dedication to preparation is enough.

Dinner: Collective preparation ensues tragedy.

Snack: Judging preparation is one of the easiest things to do.

Misplaced Focus		Negative Result	Redirected Focus		Positive Result
#1: Doubt	◆》	Paralysis	Presence	◆》	Passion
#2: Complacency	◆》	Pain	Engagement	◆》	Positive Expectation
#3 Blame	◆》	Powerlessness/ Problems	Resourcefulness	◆》	Possibilities
#4 Indecision	◆》	Procrastination	Action	◆》	Progress
#5: Selfishness	◆》	Guilt	Service	◆》	Peace of Mind

DAY 83

Breakfast: Preparation should be mission driven.

Lunch: Service to a cause bigger than self is preparation of love.

Dinner: A grudge not acknowledged during preparation is a seed of confusion.

Snack: The biggest issues of the world are the smallest steps to preparation.

Misplaced Focus		Negative Result	Redirected Focus		Positive Result
#1: Doubt	◆»	Paralysis	Presence	◆»	Passion
#2: Complacency	◆»	Pain	Engagement	◆»	Positive Expectation
#3 Blame	◆»	Powerlessness/ Problems	Resourcefulness	◆»	Possibilities
#4 Indecision	◆»	Procrastination	Action	◆»	Progress
#5: Selfishness	◆»	Guilt	Service	◆»	Peace of Mind

DAY 84

Breakfast: Social Security is an example of timeless preparation.

Lunch: Your response to any situation is energy given to the preparation of order or chaos.

Dinner: Praise the unfortunate events that forced preparation as a reasonable option of operation.

Snack: The ugly truth is that preparation is impossible.

Misplaced Focus		Negative Result	Redirected Focus		Positive Result
#1: Doubt	◈»	Paralysis	Presence	◈»	Passion
#2: Complacency	◈»	Pain	Engagement	◈»	Positive Expectation
#3 Blame	◈»	Powerlessness/ Problems	Resourcefulness	◈»	Possibilities
#4 Indecision	◈»	Procrastination	Action	◈»	Progress
#5: Selfishness	◈»	Guilt	Service	◈»	Peace of Mind

DAY 85

Breakfast: Inspiration, motivation, and desperation are all mistakes of preparation.

Lunch: Enough preparation has been done.

Dinner: Eat alone until your preparation introduces you to reality.

Snack: The ultimate preparation is to knowingly yield.

Misplaced Focus		Negative Result	Redirected Focus		Positive Result
#1: Doubt	◆》	Paralysis	Presence	◆》	Passion
#2: Complacency	◆》	Pain	Engagement	◆》	Positive Expectation
#3 Blame	◆》	Powerlessness/ Problems	Resourcefulness	◆》	Possibilities
#4 Indecision	◆》	Procrastination	Action	◆》	Progress
#5: Selfishness	◆》	Guilt	Service	◆》	Peace of Mind

DAY 86

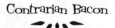

Breakfast: All preparation is not created equal.

Lunch: A true test of preparation has no teacher.

Dinner: Writing about preparation helps with the actual process.

Snack: There are many different meanings of preparation.

Misplaced Focus		Negative Result	Redirected Focus		Positive Result
#1: Doubt	◆≫	Paralysis	Presence	◆≫	Passion
#2: Complacency	◆≫	Pain	Engagement	◆≫	Positive Expectation
#3 Blame	◆≫	Powerlessness/ Problems	Resourcefulness	◆≫	Possibilities
#4 Indecision	◆≫	Procrastination	Action	◆≫	Progress
#5: Selfishness	◆≫	Guilt	Service	◆≫	Peace of Mind

DAY 87

Breakfast: A preparation mindset is one that is unplugged from influence.

Lunch: Preparation is an awakening.

Dinner: Meaningful personal discovery is the second language of preparation.

Snack: If excuses had an advantage preparation would be useless.

Misplaced Focus		Negative Result	Redirected Focus		Positive Result
#1: Doubt	◆》	Paralysis	Presence	◆》	Passion
#2: Complacency	◆》	Pain	Engagement	◆》	Positive Expectation
#3 Blame	◆》	Powerlessness/ Problems	Resourcefulness	◆》	Possibilities
#4 Indecision	◆》	Procrastination	Action	◆》	Progress
#5: Selfishness	◆》	Guilt	Service	◆》	Peace of Mind

DAY 88

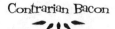

Breakfast: Not all visually appealing things require preparation.

Lunch: When preparation wanders, the universe experiences time warps.

Dinner: Anything better than preparation has identity issues.

Snack: To whom it may concern, cheating preparation does not last.

Misplaced Focus	Negative Result	Redirected Focus	Positive Result
#1: Doubt	Paralysis	Presence	Passion
#2: Complacency	Pain	Engagement	Positive Expectation
#3 Blame	Powerlessness/ Problems	Resourcefulness	Possibilities
#4 Indecision	Procrastination	Action	Progress
#5: Selfishness	Guilt	Service	Peace of Mind

DAY 89

Breakfast: Preparation is the only idea that has found success and kept looking.

Lunch: Arrival is cause for preparation.

Dinner: Basic preparation has no standards.

Snack: Signature preparation is priceless.

Misplaced Focus		Negative Result	Redirected Focus		Positive Result
#1: Doubt	◆》	Paralysis	Presence	◆》	Passion
#2: Complacency	◆》	Pain	Engagement	◆》	Positive Expectation
#3 Blame	◆》	Powerlessness/ Problems	Resourcefulness	◆》	Possibilities
#4 Indecision	◆》	Procrastination	Action	◆》	Progress
#5: Selfishness	◆》	Guilt	Service	◆》	Peace of Mind

DAY 90

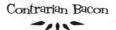

Breakfast: If you just want to travel and enjoy life, preparation is your best bet.

Lunch: In a perfect world honest preparation would be enough.

Dinner: Preparation is waiting while working.

Snack: Pricing anything capable of taking life is poor preparation.

Misplaced Focus		Negative Result	Redirected Focus		Positive Result
#1: Doubt	◆》	Paralysis	Presence	◆》	Passion
#2: Complacency	◆》	Pain	Engagement	◆》	Positive Expectation
#3 Blame	◆》	Powerlessness/ Problems	Resourcefulness	◆》	Possibilities
#4 Indecision	◆》	Procrastination	Action	◆》	Progress
#5: Selfishness	◆》	Guilt	Service	◆》	Peace of Mind

DAY 91

Breakfast: Preparation magnifies incompetence.

Lunch: Choosing between stability of preparation is 100% personal preference.

Dinner: Dodging preparation is a fun game until you get hit by life.

Snack: The brightest star is no better at preparation than the moon.

Misplaced Focus		Negative Result	Redirected Focus		Positive Result
#1: Doubt	◆》	Paralysis	Presence	◆》	Passion
#2: Complacency	◆》	Pain	Engagement	◆》	Positive Expectation
#3 Blame	◆》	Powerlessness/ Problems	Resourcefulness	◆》	Possibilities
#4 Indecision	◆》	Procrastination	Action	◆》	Progress
#5: Selfishness	◆》	Guilt	Service	◆》	Peace of Mind

DAY 92

Breakfast: Being easily bothered helps the competition with preparation.

Lunch: Limiting belief systems are created by false preparation.

Dinner: Preparation takes forever.

Snack: Evidence of preparation is found by challenging standards.

Misplaced Focus		Negative Result	Redirected Focus		Positive Result
#1: Doubt	◆》	Paralysis	Presence	◆》	Passion
#2: Complacency	◆》	Pain	Engagement	◆》	Positive Expectation
#3 Blame	◆》	Powerlessness/ Problems	Resourcefulness	◆》	Possibilities
#4 Indecision	◆》	Procrastination	Action	◆》	Progress
#5: Selfishness	◆》	Guilt	Service	◆》	Peace of Mind

DAY 93

Breakfast: Preparation is likely the only thing stopping you.

Lunch: Sometimes words like preparation make no sense.

Dinner: Careless preparation can ruin the same lives it saves.

Snack: Independence anchors preparation.

Misplaced Focus		Negative Result	Redirected Focus		Positive Result
#1: Doubt	◆》	Paralysis	Presence	◆》	Passion
#2: Complacency	◆》	Pain	Engagement	◆》	Positive Expectation
#3 Blame	◆》	Powerlessness/ Problems	Resourcefulness	◆》	Possibilities
#4 Indecision	◆》	Procrastination	Action	◆》	Progress
#5: Selfishness	◆》	Guilt	Service	◆》	Peace of Mind

DAY 94

Breakfast: Preparation calendars would be nice.

Lunch: Preparation is the delicate balance between greed and hunger.

Dinner: Personification of preparation is mentally draining.

Snack: Preparation allows you to write yourself into history anyway you want.

Misplaced Focus		Negative Result	Redirected Focus		Positive Result
#1: Doubt	»	Paralysis	Presence	»	Passion
#2: Complacency	»	Pain	Engagement	»	Positive Expectation
#3 Blame	»	Powerlessness/ Problems	Resourcefulness	»	Possibilities
#4 Indecision	»	Procrastination	Action	»	Progress
#5: Selfishness	»	Guilt	Service	»	Peace of Mind

DAY 95

Breakfast: If your future doesn't excite you, preparation won't either.

Lunch: If it feels right don't let preparation slow you down.

Dinner: The people who don't care about preparation make the biggest waves.

Snack: Maintaining an image is a perfect waste of preparation.

Misplaced Focus		Negative Result	Redirected Focus		Positive Result
#1: Doubt	◆》	Paralysis	Presence	◆》	Passion
#2: Complacency	◆》	Pain	Engagement	◆》	Positive Expectation
#3 Blame	◆》	Powerlessness/ Problems	Resourcefulness	◆》	Possibilities
#4 Indecision	◆》	Procrastination	Action	◆》	Progress
#5: Selfishness	◆》	Guilt	Service	◆》	Peace of Mind

DAY 96

Breakfast: Learning requires more preparation than anything else.

Lunch: Preparation does not need to take massive action.

Dinner: Cake is preparation for pleasure.

Snack: Laughter is the best preparation for pain.

Misplaced Focus		Negative Result	Redirected Focus		Positive Result
#1: Doubt	◆》	Paralysis	Presence	◆》	Passion
#2: Complacency	◆》	Pain	Engagement	◆》	Positive Expectation
#3 Blame	◆》	Powerlessness/ Problems	Resourcefulness	◆》	Possibilities
#4 Indecision	◆》	Procrastination	Action	◆》	Progress
#5: Selfishness	◆》	Guilt	Service	◆》	Peace of Mind

DAY 97

Breakfast: The biggest benefit of preparation is choice.

Lunch: Cigarettes are preparation.

Dinner: Preparation is a dance of decisions.

Snack: Arguments against preparation are the truth.

Misplaced Focus		Negative Result	Redirected Focus		Positive Result
#1: Doubt	◆》	Paralysis	Presence	◆》	Passion
#2: Complacency	◆》	Pain	Engagement	◆》	Positive Expectation
#3 Blame	◆》	Powerlessness/ Problems	Resourcefulness	◆》	Possibilities
#4 Indecision	◆》	Procrastination	Action	◆》	Progress
#5: Selfishness	◆》	Guilt	Service	◆》	Peace of Mind

DAY 98

Breakfast: If you know how old people think, preparation is free money.

Lunch: A calculated risk is worth the preparation.

Dinner: To a farmer the egg is the best excuse preparation has ever seen.

Snack: Preparation has seen a decline since convenience.

Misplaced Focus		Negative Result	Redirected Focus		Positive Result
#1: Doubt	◆》	Paralysis	Presence	◆》	Passion
#2: Complacency	◆》	Pain	Engagement	◆》	Positive Expectation
#3 Blame	◆》	Powerlessness/ Problems	Resourcefulness	◆》	Possibilities
#4 Indecision	◆》	Procrastination	Action	◆》	Progress
#5: Selfishness	◆》	Guilt	Service	◆》	Peace of Mind

DAY 99

Breakfast: Luck is a random act of preparation.

Lunch: Preparation of depression is favorable circumstances and smiling faces.

Dinner: Elections are blind preparation.

Snack: A job is preparation for jealousy.

Misplaced Focus		Negative Result	Redirected Focus		Positive Result
#1: Doubt	◆》	Paralysis	Presence	◆》	Passion
#2: Complacency	◆》	Pain	Engagement	◆》	Positive Expectation
#3 Blame	◆》	Powerlessness/ Problems	Resourcefulness	◆》	Possibilities
#4 Indecision	◆》	Procrastination	Action	◆》	Progress
#5: Selfishness	◆》	Guilt	Service	◆》	Peace of Mind

DAY 100

Breakfast: Fantasy is the king of preparation.

Lunch: A guideline is preparation for attention.

Dinner: Rules break preparation.

Snack: Preparation is just the start button.

Misplaced Focus		Negative Result	Redirected Focus		Positive Result
#1: Doubt	◆》	Paralysis	Presence	◆》	Passion
#2: Complacency	◆》	Pain	Engagement	◆》	Positive Expectation
#3 Blame	◆》	Powerlessness/ Problems	Resourcefulness	◆》	Possibilities
#4 Indecision	◆》	Procrastination	Action	◆》	Progress
#5: Selfishness	◆》	Guilt	Service	◆》	Peace of Mind

65 Days of Action

The Contrarian's Solution

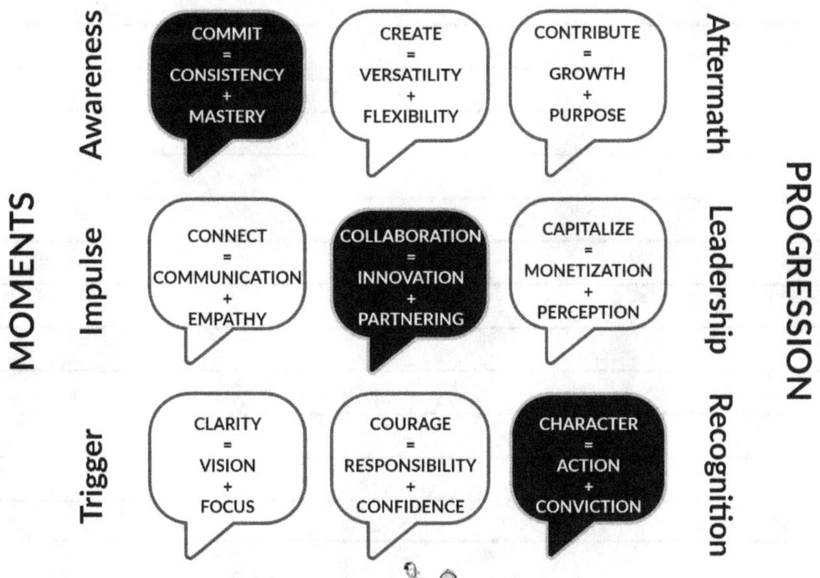

Contrarian
Bacon

DAY 1

Breakfast: Action is the least likely to solve conflict.

Lunch: Indirect action sustains legacies.

Dinner: Purposeful action builds momentum.

Snack: If you want to light yourself on fire with purpose, good, but don't expect everyone to understand and take action also.

Misplaced Focus		Negative Result	Redirected Focus		Positive Result
#1: Doubt	◆》	Paralysis	Presence	◆》	Passion
#2: Complacency	◆》	Pain	Engagement	◆》	Positive Expectation
#3 Blame	◆》	Powerlessness/ Problems	Resourcefulness	◆》	Possibilities
#4 Indecision	◆》	Procrastination	Action	◆》	Progress
#5: Selfishness	◆》	Guilt	Service	◆》	Peace of Mind

DAY 2

Breakfast: Action or anonymity—both are equally useful.

Lunch: If ever an action was needed, it would be painfully obvious.

Dinner: It makes more sense to train flying insects than to force action.

Snack: Quitters are good at taking the first and biggest action.

Misplaced Focus	Negative Result	Redirected Focus	Positive Result
#1: Doubt	Paralysis	Presence	Passion
#2: Complacency	Pain	Engagement	Positive Expectation
#3 Blame	Powerlessness/ Problems	Resourcefulness	Possibilities
#4 Indecision	Procrastination	Action	Progress
#5: Selfishness	Guilt	Service	Peace of Mind

DAY 3

Breakfast: Deliberate inaction is an action worth observing more closely.

Lunch: The action of blaming anyone is a waste of time and corrective energy.

Dinner: A small action can symbolize eternity.

Snack: Strength is proof that action serves a definite purpose.

Misplaced Focus		Negative Result	Redirected Focus		Positive Result
#1: Doubt	◆》	Paralysis	Presence	◆》	Passion
#2: Complacency	◆》	Pain	Engagement	◆》	Positive Expectation
#3 Blame	◆》	Powerlessness/ Problems	Resourcefulness	◆》	Possibilities
#4 Indecision	◆》	Procrastination	Action	◆》	Progress
#5: Selfishness	◆》	Guilt	Service	◆》	Peace of Mind

DAY 4

Breakfast: Children should be allowed to take any action they want—in a cage.

Lunch: Clueless action deserves the death penalty.

Dinner: Long lasting action is either senseless or an emergency.

Snack: Approach action as if it were the first time.

Misplaced Focus		Negative Result	Redirected Focus		Positive Result
#1: Doubt	⟫	Paralysis	Presence	⟫	Passion
#2: Complacency	⟫	Pain	Engagement	⟫	Positive Expectation
#3 Blame	⟫	Powerlessness/ Problems	Resourcefulness	⟫	Possibilities
#4 Indecision	⟫	Procrastination	Action	⟫	Progress
#5: Selfishness	⟫	Guilt	Service	⟫	Peace of Mind

DAY 5

Breakfast: Proper order is the action of success.

Lunch: The concept of action is knowingly flawed—along with feelings.

Dinner: The action I take will be in the form of a question; What if I'm wrong?

Snack: It is action that makes a name.

Misplaced Focus		Negative Result	Redirected Focus		Positive Result
#1: Doubt	◈»	Paralysis	Presence	◈»	Passion
#2: Complacency	◈»	Pain	Engagement	◈»	Positive Expectation
#3 Blame	◈»	Powerlessness/ Problems	Resourcefulness	◈»	Possibilities
#4 Indecision	◈»	Procrastination	Action	◈»	Progress
#5: Selfishness	◈»	Guilt	Service	◈»	Peace of Mind

DAY 6

Breakfast: Action enhanced by glory is service.

Lunch: The results of action and knowledge are well documented.

Dinner: Favorable action is just an idea.

Snack: A mistake caused by action can be easily hidden.

Misplaced Focus	Negative Result	Redirected Focus	Positive Result
#1: Doubt	Paralysis	Presence	Passion
#2: Complacency	Pain	Engagement	Positive Expectation
#3 Blame	Powerlessness/ Problems	Resourcefulness	Possibilities
#4 Indecision	Procrastination	Action	Progress
#5: Selfishness	Guilt	Service	Peace of Mind

DAY 7

Breakfast: Individual action is feared from a distance and appreciated in close encounters.

Lunch: Action filtered through anything is confusion.

Dinner: If action were about patience, some things would never be finished.

Snack: Action is not a cure, it is action.

Misplaced Focus		Negative Result	Redirected Focus		Positive Result
#1: Doubt	◆》	Paralysis	Presence	◆》	Passion
#2: Complacency	◆》	Pain	Engagement	◆》	Positive Expectation
#3 Blame	◆》	Powerlessness/ Problems	Resourcefulness	◆》	Possibilities
#4 Indecision	◆》	Procrastination	Action	◆》	Progress
#5: Selfishness	◆》	Guilt	Service	◆》	Peace of Mind

DAY 8

Breakfast: From the outside all action seems risky.

Lunch: Taking daily action is a good starting point, but eventually the days are no more useful than wet socks.

Dinner: Consistency neutralizes action.

Snack: When a well-known artist takes action, it is usually referred to as a masterpiece.

Misplaced Focus		Negative Result	Redirected Focus		Positive Result
#1: Doubt	⟫	Paralysis	Presence	⟫	Passion
#2: Complacency	⟫	Pain	Engagement	⟫	Positive Expectation
#3 Blame	⟫	Powerlessness/ Problems	Resourcefulness	⟫	Possibilities
#4 Indecision	⟫	Procrastination	Action	⟫	Progress
#5: Selfishness	⟫	Guilt	Service	⟫	Peace of Mind

DAY 9

Breakfast: Action without collective approval is a potential threat to culture.

Lunch: Action that disregards sacrifice is foolish behavior.

Dinner: New action is not always good action.

Snack: Action is a glimpse of everything it takes to create change.

Misplaced Focus		Negative Result	Redirected Focus		Positive Result
#1: Doubt	◆》	Paralysis	Presence	◆》	Passion
#2: Complacency	◆》	Pain	Engagement	◆》	Positive Expectation
#3 Blame	◆》	Powerlessness/ Problems	Resourcefulness	◆》	Possibilities
#4 Indecision	◆》	Procrastination	Action	◆》	Progress
#5: Selfishness	◆》	Guilt	Service	◆》	Peace of Mind

DAY 10

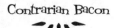

Breakfast: A plan of action that still produces uncertainty lacks persistence.

Lunch: Building an organizational structure independent of constant action creates equality.

Dinner: Action is a legitimate competitor of time.

Snack: Laziness as an action has surprising benefits.

Misplaced Focus	Negative Result	Redirected Focus	Positive Result
#1: Doubt	Paralysis	Presence	Passion
#2: Complacency	Pain	Engagement	Positive Expectation
#3 Blame	Powerlessness/ Problems	Resourcefulness	Possibilities
#4 Indecision	Procrastination	Action	Progress
#5: Selfishness	Guilt	Service	Peace of Mind

DAY 11

Breakfast: I want my action to be challenged by my offspring.

Lunch: Actual security requires very little action.

Dinner: Action is the difference between $50K a year and $50K a month.

Snack: Delayed action is a good strategy.

Misplaced Focus		Negative Result	Redirected Focus		Positive Result
#1: Doubt	◆》	Paralysis	Presence	◆》	Passion
#2: Complacency	◆》	Pain	Engagement	◆》	Positive Expectation
#3 Blame	◆》	Powerlessness/ Problems	Resourcefulness	◆》	Possibilities
#4 Indecision	◆》	Procrastination	Action	◆》	Progress
#5: Selfishness	◆》	Guilt	Service	◆》	Peace of Mind

DAY 12

Breakfast: A divorce from action is compliance with low standards.

Lunch: A world of action is entertaining but elementary.

Dinner: Waiting to take action shows restraint which can also be weakness.

Snack: The simplest action that can be taken in difficult times is thought.

Misplaced Focus		Negative Result	Redirected Focus		Positive Result
#1: Doubt	◆》	Paralysis	Presence	◆》	Passion
#2: Complacency	◆》	Pain	Engagement	◆》	Positive Expectation
#3 Blame	◆》	Powerlessness/ Problems	Resourcefulness	◆》	Possibilities
#4 Indecision	◆》	Procrastination	Action	◆》	Progress
#5: Selfishness	◆》	Guilt	Service	◆》	Peace of Mind

DAY 13

Breakfast: Calling an action unintended is reckless endangerment.

Lunch: Reflection without intentional action is false representation.

Dinner: Direct deposit is the only action that excites me.

Snack: Action is the secret to any lasting formula.

Misplaced Focus		Negative Result	Redirected Focus		Positive Result
#1: Doubt	◆》	Paralysis	Presence	◆》	Passion
#2: Complacency	◆》	Pain	Engagement	◆》	Positive Expectation
#3 Blame	◆》	Powerlessness/ Problems	Resourcefulness	◆》	Possibilities
#4 Indecision	◆》	Procrastination	Action	◆》	Progress
#5: Selfishness	◆》	Guilt	Service	◆》	Peace of Mind

DAY 14

Breakfast: Violent action has no end.

Lunch: Taking inventory is a smooth action.

Dinner: The useful action of learning new things is continuation of worthwhile beliefs.

Snack: Action that heals is always worth it.

Misplaced Focus		Negative Result	Redirected Focus		Positive Result
#1: Doubt	◆»	Paralysis	Presence	◆»	Passion
#2: Complacency	◆»	Pain	Engagement	◆»	Positive Expectation
#3 Blame	◆»	Powerlessness/ Problems	Resourcefulness	◆»	Possibilities
#4 Indecision	◆»	Procrastination	Action	◆»	Progress
#5: Selfishness	◆»	Guilt	Service	◆»	Peace of Mind

DAY 15

Breakfast: Action helps just about everything.

Lunch: Unannounced action has a special place in the universe.

Dinner: Action is belief in faith.

Snack: Hyping action up should be left to encouragement.

Misplaced Focus		Negative Result	Redirected Focus		Positive Result
#1: Doubt	◆》	Paralysis	Presence	◆》	Passion
#2: Complacency	◆》	Pain	Engagement	◆》	Positive Expectation
#3 Blame	◆》	Powerlessness/ Problems	Resourcefulness	◆》	Possibilities
#4 Indecision	◆》	Procrastination	Action	◆》	Progress
#5: Selfishness	◆》	Guilt	Service	◆》	Peace of Mind

DAY 16

Breakfast: Action that sells is action that fails.

Lunch: Competitive action is essential but wasteful.

Dinner: Corrective action should be given, not taken.

Snack: Being scared into action can sink ships or save nations—depends on the weather.

Misplaced Focus		Negative Result	Redirected Focus		Positive Result
#1: Doubt	»	Paralysis	Presence	»	Passion
#2: Complacency	»	Pain	Engagement	»	Positive Expectation
#3 Blame	»	Powerlessness/ Problems	Resourcefulness	»	Possibilities
#4 Indecision	»	Procrastination	Action	»	Progress
#5: Selfishness	»	Guilt	Service	»	Peace of Mind

DAY 17

Breakfast: Understanding action before going full throttle is the new vibe.

Lunch: Take a break if you need to, but don't quit taking action towards peace of mind.

Dinner: Action sleeps standing up.

Snack: After the seed is planted, action is still needed.

Misplaced Focus		Negative Result	Redirected Focus		Positive Result
#1: Doubt	◆》	Paralysis	Presence	◆》	Passion
#2: Complacency	◆》	Pain	Engagement	◆》	Positive Expectation
#3 Blame	◆》	Powerlessness/ Problems	Resourcefulness	◆》	Possibilities
#4 Indecision	◆》	Procrastination	Action	◆》	Progress
#5: Selfishness	◆》	Guilt	Service	◆》	Peace of Mind

DAY 18

Breakfast: Hope comes from action.

Lunch: Action is the primary catalyst to character.

Dinner: There are only so many words in the English language; put the ones that matter most to you into action.

Snack: Supporting action without research is more damaging than global warming.

Misplaced Focus	Negative Result	Redirected Focus	Positive Result
#1: Doubt	Paralysis	Presence	Passion
#2: Complacency	Pain	Engagement	Positive Expectation
#3 Blame	Powerlessness/ Problems	Resourcefulness	Possibilities
#4 Indecision	Procrastination	Action	Progress
#5: Selfishness	Guilt	Service	Peace of Mind

DAY 19

Breakfast: Excessive action seems like a good idea, but if everybody bought into it home life would be ruined.

Lunch: Figurative reversal of an action helps no one.

Dinner: Wishful thinking is cute, but are you willing to take action?

Snack: The consequences of action all have the same father.

Misplaced Focus		Negative Result	Redirected Focus		Positive Result
#1: Doubt	◆》	Paralysis	Presence	◆》	Passion
#2: Complacency	◆》	Pain	Engagement	◆》	Positive Expectation
#3 Blame	◆》	Powerlessness/ Problems	Resourcefulness	◆》	Possibilities
#4 Indecision	◆》	Procrastination	Action	◆》	Progress
#5: Selfishness	◆》	Guilt	Service	◆》	Peace of Mind

DAY 20

Breakfast: At the top action is mandatory.

Lunch: At the bottom action is optional.

Dinner: In the middle action is a mistake.

Snack: All around, action can't be faked.

Misplaced Focus	Negative Result	Redirected Focus	Positive Result
#1: Doubt	Paralysis	Presence	Passion
#2: Complacency	Pain	Engagement	Positive Expectation
#3 Blame	Powerlessness/ Problems	Resourcefulness	Possibilities
#4 Indecision	Procrastination	Action	Progress
#5: Selfishness	Guilt	Service	Peace of Mind

DAY 21

Breakfast: With enough action time takes a break.

Lunch: Action consumes confusion.

Dinner: The lifetime value of action takers exceeds imagination.

Snack: Action is part of the process where talking should end.

Misplaced Focus	Negative Result	Redirected Focus	Positive Result
#1: Doubt	Paralysis	Presence	Passion
#2: Complacency	Pain	Engagement	Positive Expectation
#3 Blame	Powerlessness/ Problems	Resourcefulness	Possibilities
#4 Indecision	Procrastination	Action	Progress
#5: Selfishness	Guilt	Service	Peace of Mind

DAY 22

Breakfast: The art of action is widely appreciated.

Lunch: If there is no action in the market, the world has ended.

Dinner: Action is not a contest; it is a tool for survival.

Snack: Take your own action and use your own words.

Misplaced Focus		Negative Result	Redirected Focus		Positive Result
#1: Doubt	◆》	Paralysis	Presence	◆》	Passion
#2: Complacency	◆》	Pain	Engagement	◆》	Positive Expectation
#3 Blame	◆》	Powerlessness/ Problems	Resourcefulness	◆》	Possibilities
#4 Indecision	◆》	Procrastination	Action	◆》	Progress
#5: Selfishness	◆》	Guilt	Service	◆》	Peace of Mind

DAY 23

Breakfast: When no action is needed, get drunk.

Lunch: Extreme action is a puzzle with missing pieces.

Dinner: Unregulated action for some strange reason scares people.

Snack: The stimulant of revelation is action.

Misplaced Focus		Negative Result	Redirected Focus		Positive Result
#1: Doubt	◆》	Paralysis	Presence	◆》	Passion
#2: Complacency	◆》	Pain	Engagement	◆》	Positive Expectation
#3 Blame	◆》	Powerlessness/ Problems	Resourcefulness	◆》	Possibilities
#4 Indecision	◆》	Procrastination	Action	◆》	Progress
#5: Selfishness	◆》	Guilt	Service	◆》	Peace of Mind

DAY 24

Breakfast: Full creative control requires no action.

Lunch: Desperate action is usually filled with guilt.

Dinner: Seeking action for gain loses attention.

Snack: Following takes just as much action as leading.

Misplaced Focus		Negative Result	Redirected Focus		Positive Result
#1: Doubt	◆»	Paralysis	Presence	◆»	Passion
#2: Complacency	◆»	Pain	Engagement	◆»	Positive Expectation
#3 Blame	◆»	Powerlessness/ Problems	Resourcefulness	◆»	Possibilities
#4 Indecision	◆»	Procrastination	Action	◆»	Progress
#5: Selfishness	◆»	Guilt	Service	◆»	Peace of Mind

DAY 25

Breakfast: Action crowds many spaces with regret.

Lunch: A missed opportunity is a good excuse to take action.

Dinner: Isolation of action allows truth to operate.

Snack: Right action feels wrong when rushing.

Misplaced Focus		Negative Result	Redirected Focus		Positive Result
#1: Doubt	◆》	Paralysis	Presence	◆》	Passion
#2: Complacency	◆》	Pain	Engagement	◆》	Positive Expectation
#3 Blame	◆》	Powerlessness/ Problems	Resourcefulness	◆》	Possibilities
#4 Indecision	◆》	Procrastination	Action	◆》	Progress
#5: Selfishness	◆》	Guilt	Service	◆》	Peace of Mind

DAY 26

Breakfast: Any special actions taken to avoid misunderstanding simply must not occur.

Lunch: Action is a choice to not settle for current circumstances.

Dinner: The struggle bus uses action for fuel.

Snack: Hidden action builds tension.

Misplaced Focus		Negative Result	Redirected Focus		Positive Result
#1: Doubt	»	Paralysis	Presence	»	Passion
#2: Complacency	»	Pain	Engagement	»	Positive Expectation
#3 Blame	»	Powerlessness/ Problems	Resourcefulness	»	Possibilities
#4 Indecision	»	Procrastination	Action	»	Progress
#5: Selfishness	»	Guilt	Service	»	Peace of Mind

DAY 27

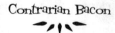

Breakfast: The more you do, the more action seems like the answer to any prayer.

Lunch: Rushed action has little benefit after birth.

Dinner: Responsible action helps guide those who need it.

Snack: Action experts can't stop.

Misplaced Focus		Negative Result	Redirected Focus		Positive Result
#1: Doubt	◆》	Paralysis	Presence	◆》	Passion
#2: Complacency	◆》	Pain	Engagement	◆》	Positive Expectation
#3 Blame	◆》	Powerlessness/ Problems	Resourcefulness	◆》	Possibilities
#4 Indecision	◆》	Procrastination	Action	◆》	Progress
#5: Selfishness	◆》	Guilt	Service	◆》	Peace of Mind

DAY 28

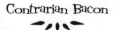

Breakfast: Mundane action connects with the birds.

Lunch: Action plays a key role in life on Mondays.

Dinner: The amount of action taken shows up in the results produced.

Snack: Happiness found in action will likely last.

Misplaced Focus		Negative Result	Redirected Focus		Positive Result
#1: Doubt	◆》	Paralysis	Presence	◆》	Passion
#2: Complacency	◆》	Pain	Engagement	◆》	Positive Expectation
#3 Blame	◆》	Powerlessness/ Problems	Resourcefulness	◆》	Possibilities
#4 Indecision	◆》	Procrastination	Action	◆》	Progress
#5: Selfishness	◆》	Guilt	Service	◆》	Peace of Mind

DAY 29

Breakfast: Anything compared to action becomes conflict.

Lunch: Slow and steady action reveals true intentions.

Dinner: Action based theory has been around forever.

Snack: Action inside a comfort zone lives off pizza.

Misplaced Focus		Negative Result	Redirected Focus		Positive Result
#1: Doubt	◆》	Paralysis	Presence	◆》	Passion
#2: Complacency	◆》	Pain	Engagement	◆》	Positive Expectation
#3 Blame	◆》	Powerlessness/ Problems	Resourcefulness	◆》	Possibilities
#4 Indecision	◆》	Procrastination	Action	◆》	Progress
#5: Selfishness	◆》	Guilt	Service	◆》	Peace of Mind

DAY 30

Breakfast: Action used as a judgement device is like prejudice.

Lunch: Assignment of titles is a one sided action.

Dinner: When the action taken has zero impact, success has been weaponized.

Snack: A system with little to no action worries worriers and rewards warriors.

Misplaced Focus		Negative Result	Redirected Focus		Positive Result
#1: Doubt	»	Paralysis	Presence	»	Passion
#2: Complacency	»	Pain	Engagement	»	Positive Expectation
#3 Blame	»	Powerlessness/ Problems	Resourcefulness	»	Possibilities
#4 Indecision	»	Procrastination	Action	»	Progress
#5: Selfishness	»	Guilt	Service	»	Peace of Mind

DAY 31

Breakfast: Solving a problem with medicine is a costly action cheat code.

Lunch: Education used in action saves lives.

Dinner: The deepest feeling of sorrow is produced by life action.

Snack: You never know how bad somebody wants
to win until action becomes necessity.

Misplaced Focus		Negative Result	Redirected Focus		Positive Result
#1: Doubt	◆》	Paralysis	Presence	◆》	Passion
#2: Complacency	◆》	Pain	Engagement	◆》	Positive Expectation
#3 Blame	◆》	Powerlessness/ Problems	Resourcefulness	◆》	Possibilities
#4 Indecision	◆》	Procrastination	Action	◆》	Progress
#5: Selfishness	◆》	Guilt	Service	◆》	Peace of Mind

DAY 32

Breakfast: Action can touch invisibility.

Lunch: When action meets limitation, it is welcomed by struggle.

Dinner: A circus is pure action.

Snack: A loss in action is a win in execution.

Misplaced Focus		Negative Result	Redirected Focus		Positive Result
#1: Doubt	»	Paralysis	Presence	»	Passion
#2: Complacency	»	Pain	Engagement	»	Positive Expectation
#3 Blame	»	Powerlessness/ Problems	Resourcefulness	»	Possibilities
#4 Indecision	»	Procrastination	Action	»	Progress
#5: Selfishness	»	Guilt	Service	»	Peace of Mind

DAY 33

Breakfast: Action angers most intelligent people.

Lunch: Pivoting action can be a slippery slope.

Dinner: When nothing is working right, the root cause revolves around quality of action.

Snack: Action burns the same bridges it builds and still has friends.

Misplaced Focus	Negative Result	Redirected Focus	Positive Result
#1: Doubt	Paralysis	Presence	Passion
#2: Complacency	Pain	Engagement	Positive Expectation
#3 Blame	Powerlessness/ Problems	Resourcefulness	Possibilities
#4 Indecision	Procrastination	Action	Progress
#5: Selfishness	Guilt	Service	Peace of Mind

DAY 34

Breakfast: Free speech is an action that commonly lacks understanding.

Lunch: Advice about action is propaganda; listen politely but ignore heavily.

Dinner: Precise verbal communication is an action of honor.

Snack: Progressive action has no voice.

Misplaced Focus	Negative Result	Redirected Focus	Positive Result
#1: Doubt	Paralysis	Presence	Passion
#2: Complacency	Pain	Engagement	Positive Expectation
#3 Blame	Powerlessness/ Problems	Resourcefulness	Possibilities
#4 Indecision	Procrastination	Action	Progress
#5: Selfishness	Guilt	Service	Peace of Mind

DAY 35

Breakfast: A clear schedule simplifies efficient action.

Lunch: Fairytales are horrible situations where action does not matter.

Dinner: If action were to be brainwashed, existence would collapse.

Snack: Disposal of doubt and fear activates action.

Misplaced Focus		Negative Result	Redirected Focus		Positive Result
#1: Doubt	⟫	Paralysis	Presence	⟫	Passion
#2: Complacency	⟫	Pain	Engagement	⟫	Positive Expectation
#3 Blame	⟫	Powerlessness/ Problems	Resourcefulness	⟫	Possibilities
#4 Indecision	⟫	Procrastination	Action	⟫	Progress
#5: Selfishness	⟫	Guilt	Service	⟫	Peace of Mind

DAY 36

Breakfast: Action that translates into memory is contagious.

Lunch: Vivid action always seems new.

Dinner: Action is quite repetitive.

Snack: Focus on action—the vibes are different.

Misplaced Focus		Negative Result	Redirected Focus		Positive Result
#1: Doubt	◆》	Paralysis	Presence	◆》	Passion
#2: Complacency	◆》	Pain	Engagement	◆》	Positive Expectation
#3 Blame	◆》	Powerlessness/ Problems	Resourcefulness	◆》	Possibilities
#4 Indecision	◆》	Procrastination	Action	◆》	Progress
#5: Selfishness	◆》	Guilt	Service	◆》	Peace of Mind

DAY 37

Breakfast: Action is usually the loudest in the room.

Lunch: Spontaneous action looks foolish.

Dinner: The action of service fills a deep void.

Snack: Brain activity is action that is often overlooked.

Misplaced Focus		Negative Result	Redirected Focus		Positive Result
#1: Doubt	◆》	Paralysis	Presence	◆》	Passion
#2: Complacency	◆》	Pain	Engagement	◆》	Positive Expectation
#3 Blame	◆》	Powerlessness/ Problems	Resourcefulness	◆》	Possibilities
#4 Indecision	◆》	Procrastination	Action	◆》	Progress
#5: Selfishness	◆》	Guilt	Service	◆》	Peace of Mind

DAY 38

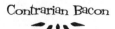

Breakfast: Oppressed action suffers from neglect.

Lunch: Guessing which action will work best is a questionable life strategy.

Dinner: Healthy action earns leisure.

Snack: Inside of action you will find peaceful rest.

Misplaced Focus		Negative Result	Redirected Focus		Positive Result
#1: Doubt	◆》	Paralysis	Presence	◆》	Passion
#2: Complacency	◆》	Pain	Engagement	◆》	Positive Expectation
#3 Blame	◆》	Powerlessness/ Problems	Resourcefulness	◆》	Possibilities
#4 Indecision	◆》	Procrastination	Action	◆》	Progress
#5: Selfishness	◆》	Guilt	Service	◆》	Peace of Mind

DAY 39

Breakfast: One kind action is all it takes to know happiness.

Lunch: Action is a natural occurrence after rest.

Dinner: The duties of action are vague.

Snack: Absence of obvious action does not mean sleep.

Misplaced Focus		Negative Result	Redirected Focus		Positive Result
#1: Doubt	◆》	Paralysis	Presence	◆》	Passion
#2: Complacency	◆》	Pain	Engagement	◆》	Positive Expectation
#3 Blame	◆》	Powerlessness/ Problems	Resourcefulness	◆》	Possibilities
#4 Indecision	◆》	Procrastination	Action	◆》	Progress
#5: Selfishness	◆》	Guilt	Service	◆》	Peace of Mind

DAY 40

Breakfast: Arrogant action has a death wish.

Lunch: Any kind of action attracts attention eventually.

Dinner: Any barrier to action is behavioral.

Snack: Calculated actions do not eliminate risk.

Misplaced Focus		Negative Result	Redirected Focus		Positive Result
#1: Doubt	◆》	Paralysis	Presence	◆》	Passion
#2: Complacency	◆》	Pain	Engagement	◆》	Positive Expectation
#3 Blame	◆》	Powerlessness/ Problems	Resourcefulness	◆》	Possibilities
#4 Indecision	◆》	Procrastination	Action	◆》	Progress
#5: Selfishness	◆》	Guilt	Service	◆》	Peace of Mind

DAY 41

Breakfast: Careful action breeds misplaced concern.

Lunch: Don't expect much public success after any type of threatening action.

Dinner: If confidence is more important than the action,
what on earth are you attempting to prove?

Snack: Emotional action should not be sustained for long periods of time.

Misplaced Focus		Negative Result	Redirected Focus		Positive Result
#1: Doubt	◆》	Paralysis	Presence	◆》	Passion
#2: Complacency	◆》	Pain	Engagement	◆》	Positive Expectation
#3 Blame	◆》	Powerlessness/ Problems	Resourcefulness	◆》	Possibilities
#4 Indecision	◆》	Procrastination	Action	◆》	Progress
#5: Selfishness	◆》	Guilt	Service	◆》	Peace of Mind

DAY 42

Breakfast: Organic action is too good to be true.

Lunch: If you can wait long enough every action has value.

Dinner: If consistency were the only action you knew, habit would be neutralized.

Snack: Action toward temptations delays positive reinforcements.

Misplaced Focus		Negative Result	Redirected Focus		Positive Result
#1: Doubt	◆》	Paralysis	Presence	◆》	Passion
#2: Complacency	◆》	Pain	Engagement	◆》	Positive Expectation
#3 Blame	◆》	Powerlessness/ Problems	Resourcefulness	◆》	Possibilities
#4 Indecision	◆》	Procrastination	Action	◆》	Progress
#5: Selfishness	◆》	Guilt	Service	◆》	Peace of Mind

DAY 43

Breakfast: Smiling is positive action.

Lunch: Action breeds more action.

Dinner: Exhaustion should not be a roadblock to action.

Snack: Soul is the source of action.

Misplaced Focus		Negative Result	Redirected Focus		Positive Result
#1: Doubt	»	Paralysis	Presence	»	Passion
#2: Complacency	»	Pain	Engagement	»	Positive Expectation
#3 Blame	»	Powerlessness/ Problems	Resourcefulness	»	Possibilities
#4 Indecision	»	Procrastination	Action	»	Progress
#5: Selfishness	»	Guilt	Service	»	Peace of Mind

DAY 44

Breakfast: Thought is action.

Lunch: Decisions made in action are subject to being more targeted.

Dinner: Calm action is not entertaining.

Snack: Action is a style like no other.

Misplaced Focus		Negative Result	Redirected Focus		Positive Result
#1: Doubt	◆》	Paralysis	Presence	◆》	Passion
#2: Complacency	◆》	Pain	Engagement	◆》	Positive Expectation
#3 Blame	◆》	Powerlessness/ Problems	Resourcefulness	◆》	Possibilities
#4 Indecision	◆》	Procrastination	Action	◆》	Progress
#5: Selfishness	◆》	Guilt	Service	◆》	Peace of Mind

DAY 45

Breakfast: With the right action, the rest of your life is already the best of your life.

Lunch: Action is cut from a different cloth.

Dinner: Not everyone will fully experience action.

Snack: Action cleans up the same disaster it causes.

Misplaced Focus		Negative Result	Redirected Focus		Positive Result
#1: Doubt	◆》	Paralysis	Presence	◆》	Passion
#2: Complacency	◆》	Pain	Engagement	◆》	Positive Expectation
#3 Blame	◆》	Powerlessness/ Problems	Resourcefulness	◆》	Possibilities
#4 Indecision	◆》	Procrastination	Action	◆》	Progress
#5: Selfishness	◆》	Guilt	Service	◆》	Peace of Mind

DAY 46

Breakfast: Don't tell them anything, show them your action.

Lunch: By default, action has the bigger audience.

Dinner: One simple action of the sun is to nourish all life.

Snack: The action of the unknown is slightly spiritual.

Misplaced Focus		Negative Result	Redirected Focus		Positive Result
#1: Doubt	◆》	Paralysis	Presence	◆》	Passion
#2: Complacency	◆》	Pain	Engagement	◆》	Positive Expectation
#3 Blame	◆》	Powerlessness/ Problems	Resourcefulness	◆》	Possibilities
#4 Indecision	◆》	Procrastination	Action	◆》	Progress
#5: Selfishness	◆》	Guilt	Service	◆》	Peace of Mind

DAY 47

Breakfast: All action should not be autonomous.

Lunch: Belief with no action dances with theory.

Dinner: The easily offended use action as a controlled substance.

Snack: Rest determines the quality of action.

Misplaced Focus		Negative Result	Redirected Focus		Positive Result
#1: Doubt	◆》	Paralysis	Presence	◆》	Passion
#2: Complacency	◆》	Pain	Engagement	◆》	Positive Expectation
#3 Blame	◆》	Powerlessness/ Problems	Resourcefulness	◆》	Possibilities
#4 Indecision	◆》	Procrastination	Action	◆》	Progress
#5: Selfishness	◆》	Guilt	Service	◆》	Peace of Mind

DAY 48

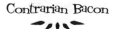

Breakfast: Trust is an action not easily explained.

Lunch: The action a hammer sees is much different than the action a saw sees.

Dinner: Action is tangible perspective.

Snack: A spoof is a story with exaggerated action.

Misplaced Focus		Negative Result	Redirected Focus		Positive Result
#1: Doubt	◆》	Paralysis	Presence	◆》	Passion
#2: Complacency	◆》	Pain	Engagement	◆》	Positive Expectation
#3 Blame	◆》	Powerlessness/ Problems	Resourcefulness	◆》	Possibilities
#4 Indecision	◆》	Procrastination	Action	◆》	Progress
#5: Selfishness	◆》	Guilt	Service	◆》	Peace of Mind

DAY 49

Breakfast: Each new level reached calls for an assessment of action.

Lunch: The quantity of action does not have to compete with the quality of action.

Dinner: Approval is wasteful action.

Snack: New beginnings forced by action have old intentions.

Misplaced Focus		Negative Result	Redirected Focus		Positive Result
#1: Doubt	◆》	Paralysis	Presence	◆》	Passion
#2: Complacency	◆》	Pain	Engagement	◆》	Positive Expectation
#3 Blame	◆》	Powerlessness/ Problems	Resourcefulness	◆》	Possibilities
#4 Indecision	◆》	Procrastination	Action	◆》	Progress
#5: Selfishness	◆》	Guilt	Service	◆》	Peace of Mind

DAY 50

Breakfast: If you ever overpay for a used car, lack of action is your problem.

Lunch: Manipulative action unfortunately works best in most situations.

Dinner: The journey from start to finish has everything to do with action.

Snack: Self guidance is reliable action.

Misplaced Focus		Negative Result	Redirected Focus		Positive Result
#1: Doubt	◆》	Paralysis	Presence	◆》	Passion
#2: Complacency	◆》	Pain	Engagement	◆》	Positive Expectation
#3 Blame	◆》	Powerlessness/ Problems	Resourcefulness	◆》	Possibilities
#4 Indecision	◆》	Procrastination	Action	◆》	Progress
#5: Selfishness	◆》	Guilt	Service	◆》	Peace of Mind

DAY 51

Breakfast: Hatred experienced personally is a painful source of action filled with emotion.

Lunch: Anniversaries are celebrations of action guided by commitment.

Dinner: Plural action is used in nightmares.

Snack: Randomly landing on an idea does not make the action process of materialization original.

Misplaced Focus	Negative Result	Redirected Focus	Positive Result
#1: Doubt	Paralysis	Presence	Passion
#2: Complacency	Pain	Engagement	Positive Expectation
#3 Blame	Powerlessness/ Problems	Resourcefulness	Possibilities
#4 Indecision	Procrastination	Action	Progress
#5: Selfishness	Guilt	Service	Peace of Mind

DAY 52

Breakfast: When action shows up as endurance, effort is conditioned to become greatness.

Lunch: Sacrificing health is a very limited action.

Dinner: Emotional intelligence is unrestricted action.

Snack: If there are no people who are surprised you're still alive, action is your only friend.

Misplaced Focus		Negative Result	Redirected Focus		Positive Result
#1: Doubt	◆》	Paralysis	Presence	◆》	Passion
#2: Complacency	◆》	Pain	Engagement	◆》	Positive Expectation
#3 Blame	◆》	Powerlessness/ Problems	Resourcefulness	◆》	Possibilities
#4 Indecision	◆》	Procrastination	Action	◆》	Progress
#5: Selfishness	◆》	Guilt	Service	◆》	Peace of Mind

DAY 53

Breakfast: Survival is primitive action.

Lunch: Legacy without action is fantasy.

Dinner: Action is the only discipline of engineering.

Snack: Characterization of anything is action based.

Misplaced Focus		Negative Result	Redirected Focus		Positive Result
#1: Doubt	◆»	Paralysis	Presence	◆»	Passion
#2: Complacency	◆»	Pain	Engagement	◆»	Positive Expectation
#3 Blame	◆»	Powerlessness/ Problems	Resourcefulness	◆»	Possibilities
#4 Indecision	◆»	Procrastination	Action	◆»	Progress
#5: Selfishness	◆»	Guilt	Service	◆»	Peace of Mind

DAY 54

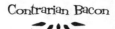

Breakfast: Action detoxes fear.

Lunch: By avoiding action, the battles only you could win get forced on others.

Dinner: Circumstance is a clear indicator regarding quality of past action.

Snack: When preservation of vices is not condemned, action becomes confusion.

Misplaced Focus		Negative Result	Redirected Focus		Positive Result
#1: Doubt	»	Paralysis	Presence	»	Passion
#2: Complacency	»	Pain	Engagement	»	Positive Expectation
#3 Blame	»	Powerlessness/ Problems	Resourcefulness	»	Possibilities
#4 Indecision	»	Procrastination	Action	»	Progress
#5: Selfishness	»	Guilt	Service	»	Peace of Mind

DAY 55

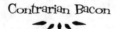

Breakfast: Energy for action is gained through forgiveness.

Lunch: Any outward advantage gained through action is not easily secured.

Dinner: One action a day keeps regret away.

Snack: Action isn't the solution to everything.

Misplaced Focus		Negative Result	Redirected Focus		Positive Result
#1: Doubt	◆》	Paralysis	Presence	◆》	Passion
#2: Complacency	◆》	Pain	Engagement	◆》	Positive Expectation
#3 Blame	◆》	Powerlessness/ Problems	Resourcefulness	◆》	Possibilities
#4 Indecision	◆》	Procrastination	Action	◆》	Progress
#5: Selfishness	◆》	Guilt	Service	◆》	Peace of Mind

DAY 56

Breakfast: The only action water needs to take is flowing.

Lunch: Wild action has its place among men.

Dinner: Action against law and order comes with certain uncertainty.

Snack: Action edits success.

Misplaced Focus		Negative Result	Redirected Focus		Positive Result
#1: Doubt	◆》	Paralysis	Presence	◆》	Passion
#2: Complacency	◆》	Pain	Engagement	◆》	Positive Expectation
#3 Blame	◆》	Powerlessness/ Problems	Resourcefulness	◆》	Possibilities
#4 Indecision	◆》	Procrastination	Action	◆》	Progress
#5: Selfishness	◆》	Guilt	Service	◆》	Peace of Mind

DAY 57

Breakfast: Game action simulates reality.

Lunch: The shadow of action operates in silence.

Dinner: Progress isn't always about action.

Snack: In the garden of action actual seeds are optional.

Misplaced Focus		Negative Result	Redirected Focus		Positive Result
#1: Doubt	◆》	Paralysis	Presence	◆》	Passion
#2: Complacency	◆》	Pain	Engagement	◆》	Positive Expectation
#3 Blame	◆》	Powerlessness/ Problems	Resourcefulness	◆》	Possibilities
#4 Indecision	◆》	Procrastination	Action	◆》	Progress
#5: Selfishness	◆》	Guilt	Service	◆》	Peace of Mind

DAY 58

Breakfast: Selling is the most useful action.

Lunch: Complaining is an infinite action.

Dinner: Training for action never ends.

Snack: Tolerating inaction is the craziest action.

Misplaced Focus		Negative Result	Redirected Focus		Positive Result
#1: Doubt	»	Paralysis	Presence	»	Passion
#2: Complacency	»	Pain	Engagement	»	Positive Expectation
#3 Blame	»	Powerlessness/ Problems	Resourcefulness	»	Possibilities
#4 Indecision	»	Procrastination	Action	»	Progress
#5: Selfishness	»	Guilt	Service	»	Peace of Mind

DAY 59

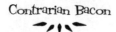

Breakfast: Action wins.

Lunch: Action<Vision.

Dinner: Action denies failure temporarily.

Snack: Responsible action violates very little.

Misplaced Focus		Negative Result	Redirected Focus		Positive Result
#1: Doubt	◆》	Paralysis	Presence	◆》	Passion
#2: Complacency	◆》	Pain	Engagement	◆》	Positive Expectation
#3 Blame	◆》	Powerlessness/ Problems	Resourcefulness	◆》	Possibilities
#4 Indecision	◆》	Procrastination	Action	◆》	Progress
#5: Selfishness	◆》	Guilt	Service	◆》	Peace of Mind

DAY 60

Breakfast: Inappropriate action has permission.

Lunch: Action does not have the best imagination.

Dinner: Failure is a planned action.

Snack: Most windows of opportunity are closed by action.

Misplaced Focus		Negative Result	Redirected Focus		Positive Result
#1: Doubt	◆»	Paralysis	Presence	◆»	Passion
#2: Complacency	◆»	Pain	Engagement	◆»	Positive Expectation
#3 Blame	◆»	Powerlessness/ Problems	Resourcefulness	◆»	Possibilities
#4 Indecision	◆»	Procrastination	Action	◆»	Progress
#5: Selfishness	◆»	Guilt	Service	◆»	Peace of Mind

DAY 61

Breakfast: Once the action stops the prices go down.

Lunch: The system of action has no positions.

Dinner: Being riddled with action is the new "I'm ready."

Snack: Action under pressure isn't always combative.

Misplaced Focus		Negative Result	Redirected Focus		Positive Result
#1: Doubt	»	Paralysis	Presence	»	Passion
#2: Complacency	»	Pain	Engagement	»	Positive Expectation
#3 Blame	»	Powerlessness/ Problems	Resourcefulness	»	Possibilities
#4 Indecision	»	Procrastination	Action	»	Progress
#5: Selfishness	»	Guilt	Service	»	Peace of Mind

DAY 62

Breakfast: The appropriate action does not always jump out at you.

Lunch: When earth takes action, we get diamonds.

Dinner: The maestro of action has no name.

Snack: If action makes you a moving target, do it with a smile.

Misplaced Focus	Negative Result	Redirected Focus	Positive Result
#1: Doubt	Paralysis	Presence	Passion
#2: Complacency	Pain	Engagement	Positive Expectation
#3 Blame	Powerlessness/ Problems	Resourcefulness	Possibilities
#4 Indecision	Procrastination	Action	Progress
#5: Selfishness	Guilt	Service	Peace of Mind

DAY 63

Breakfast: Rain makes the perfect action.

Lunch: Controlling action only creates more reason for chaos.

Dinner: Governance of action spoils time.

Snack: Fearless action is the reality of the broken.

Misplaced Focus		Negative Result	Redirected Focus		Positive Result
#1: Doubt	◆》	Paralysis	Presence	◆》	Passion
#2: Complacency	◆》	Pain	Engagement	◆》	Positive Expectation
#3 Blame	◆》	Powerlessness/ Problems	Resourcefulness	◆》	Possibilities
#4 Indecision	◆》	Procrastination	Action	◆》	Progress
#5: Selfishness	◆》	Guilt	Service	◆》	Peace of Mind

DAY 64

Breakfast: The weak-minded take action for free.

Lunch: Follow up action should always be considered.

Dinner: A life of action and adventure is optional.

Snack: Action will always be needed.

Misplaced Focus		Negative Result	Redirected Focus		Positive Result
#1: Doubt	◆》	Paralysis	Presence	◆》	Passion
#2: Complacency	◆》	Pain	Engagement	◆》	Positive Expectation
#3 Blame	◆》	Powerlessness/ Problems	Resourcefulness	◆》	Possibilities
#4 Indecision	◆》	Procrastination	Action	◆》	Progress
#5: Selfishness	◆》	Guilt	Service	◆》	Peace of Mind

DAY 65

Breakfast: The destiny of action maintains a valid driver's license.

Lunch: Biting off more than you can chew is a good action to take if you're hungry.

Dinner: Having fun should be a mandatory action.

Snack: Brave action produces story.

Misplaced Focus		Negative Result	Redirected Focus		Positive Result
#1: Doubt	◆》	Paralysis	Presence	◆》	Passion
#2: Complacency	◆》	Pain	Engagement	◆》	Positive Expectation
#3 Blame	◆》	Powerlessness/ Problems	Resourcefulness	◆》	Possibilities
#4 Indecision	◆》	Procrastination	Action	◆》	Progress
#5: Selfishness	◆》	Guilt	Service	◆》	Peace of Mind

COMPOUND INTEREST FORMULA

$$A = P\left(1 + \frac{r}{n}\right)^{nt}$$

A = final amount

P = initial principle balance

r = interest rate

n = number of times interest applied per time period

t = number of time periods elapsed

CPSIA information can be obtained
at www.ICGtesting.com
Printed in the USA
JSHW041947270921
19082JS00001B/11

9 781977 233691